# LOST LINES

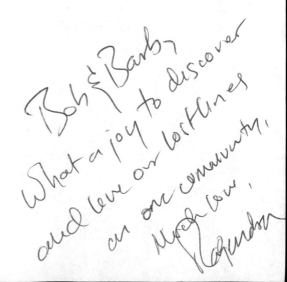

## OTHER BOOKS BY RAJ PILLAI

UNEARTHED: DISCOVER LIFE AS GOD'S MASTERPIECE

## Praise for Raj Pillai's Book *Unearthed: Discover Life as God's Masterpiece*

"Within the pages of this book you'll find thought provoking and inspiring stories that cause you to pause, reflect, and view yourself, life's events, and the world through different eyes. In a decade that has given us a cacophony of communication methods that even the most spiritually focused people cannot escape, we need to take time to stop acting like human doings and get back to what God created us to be: human beings. Through *Unearthed*, explore a quieter and more introspective world and your role in it. Working through this book alone or, as I recommend, through small group study will be a catalyst to deeper understanding of oneself, God, and others in your life. Through the lens provided within these pages by Raj Pillai, discover how each one of us is individually and collectively a true masterpiece: a work done with extraordinary skill, created and placed in the world by the one true God."

—Dr. Bettie Ann Brigham,
vice provost, Eastern University

"With a constant eye toward Scripture, Raj Pillai uses relevant examples and accessible prose to unveil the 'life that is life' and what it looks like to live into our identities as God's masterpieces."

—D. Michael Lindsay,
president, Gordon College

"Do you feel insignificant? Inadequate? Question your self-worth? Have you been wounded by what others have said about you—by what you have said about yourself? Dig deep into *Unearthed*, and you'll discover the Truth of how God sees you and the masterpiece He created you to be. Highly recommended!"

—Marlene Bagnull, author

"Even as a pastor for nearly thirty years now, one of my greatest struggles is embracing the way God made me and sees me. I know I am significant because of my position as a child of God. My worth is not in my performance or what others think of me. Knowing in your mind and believing in your heart are two different things. On a run this morning, the demons of doubt began to get the best of me again. I then sat down and read Raj's book. God's timing is always perfect. I received a jolt of energy and resolve like never before to accept that I am a masterpiece from God on an amazing journey. If you read this book, you will discover the very same thing."

—Randy Frazee,
senior minister, Oak Hills Church,
author of *Think, Act, Be like Jesus*

# LOST LINES

## A SEARCH TO FIND
## GOD'S SCRIPT
## FOR YOUR LIFE

RAJ PILLAI

NEW HOPE®
PUBLISHERS

An imprint of Iron Stream Media
Birmingham, Alabama

New Hope® Publishers
5184 Caldwell Mill Rd.
St. 204-221
Hoover, AL 35244
NewHopePublishers.com
An imprint of Iron Stream Media.

New Hope Publishers serves its authors as they express their views, which may not express the views of the
publisher.

Library of Congress Cataloging-in-Publication Data

Names: Pillai, Raj, 1968- author.
Title: Lost lines : a search to find God's script for your life / Raj Pillai.
Description: First [edition]. | Birmingham : New Hope Publishers, 2018.
Identifiers: LCCN 2018001681 | ISBN 9781625915443 (permabind)
Subjects: LCSH: Discernment (Christian theology) | God (Christianity)—Will.
 | Listening—Religious aspects—Christianity.
Classification: LCC BT135 .P49 2018 | DDC 248.4—dc23
LC record available at https://lccn.loc.gov/2018001681

Cover design by Barbara Noll.

ISBN-13: 978-1-62591-544-3

18  19  20  21  22 - - 5  4  3  2  1

# DEDICATION

Honor those leaders who work so hard for you, who have been given the responsibility of urging and guiding you along in your obedience. Overwhelm them with appreciation and love!

—*1 Thessalonians 5:12–13 The Message*

This book is dedicated
to
Mark and Huldah Buntain,
my first pastors (and Mrs. Buntain was my first boss!),
who taught me to look at the crucified Carpenter from Nazareth
for hope, for meaning, and for my life's deepest purpose.

And to
the millions of courageous local pastors,
God's faithful servants around the globe,
who work so hard staying on mission
to help people
discover their lost lines.

*Therefore,* I urge you, brothers and sisters, in view of God's mercy, to offer your bodies as a living sacrifice, holy and pleasing to God—this is your true and proper worship. Do not conform to the pattern of this world, but be transformed by the renewing of your mind. Then you will be able to test and approve what God's will is—his good, pleasing and perfect will.

*—Romans 12:1–2*

In a parable titled "The Prompter," Søren Kierkegaard once argued that people sometimes look upon the speaker at a church as an actor, and they are there to pass judgment upon him. But the speaker is not the actor, the listeners are. The speaker is the prompter, reminding them of their *lost lines*.

# CONTENTS

# LOST LINES

# OUR LOST LINES

*In* my twenty-plus years in ministry, I have given more than a thousand talks and sermons. To help me stay grounded every time I speak, I glance at the several verses, quotes, and thoughts dotting the bulletin board of my office. I have read and reread these clippings many times to inspire and remind me of my mission and why I am here.

One of the most stirring, encouraging, thought-provoking set of words I have pinned on my bulletin board is a paraphrase of words written by Danish philosopher, Søren Kierkegaard:

> **In a parable titled "The Prompter," Søren Kierkegaard
> once argued that people sometimes look upon the
> speaker at a church as an actor,
> and they are there to pass judgment upon him.
> But the speaker is not the actor, the listeners are.
> The speaker is the prompter, reminding
> them of their *lost lines*.**

These words have become a sort of personal mission statement for me. I want to remind myself, my family, and anyone I come in contact with about our lost lines.

I am giving the rest of my life to that mission. And I want to offer the rest of this book as a manifesto to why I think this mission is so critical, crucial, and compelling for our times.

*Because everyone is living a script.*

Everyone. Each one of us in our town, in our nation, in our world, is living a story. And that story has been shaped, molded, and fashioned by many things.

I care very deeply about whether we are living the right story. A lot of people in our country and our world are following a different script, a different story from the ones they were meant to live. The influence of these stories is subtle, clever, and devastating to the human soul.

And throughout history (and now through God's Word, prayer, and His community), God keeps reminding people about their lost lines.

When the Israelites crossed over the Red Sea, God told Moses to gather His people and remind them of their lost lines. That they were slaves in Egypt, living a script of oppression trapped in an identity of slavery. But those were not their true lines. God's script for Israel was to become a holy kingdom of priests, walking closely with God and living their lost lines (Exodus 19—24). Some chose to live their lost lines. But many others soon began to live a different script with tragic consequences.

When the Israelites were ready to enter the Promised Land after forty years in the desert, Moses once again reminded them of their lost lines and encouraged them live them boldly. He instructed the Israelites to not only live their own lost lines but to teach their children about their lost lines. Knowing how prone people are to forget, Moses commanded them to read the law every seven years (Deuteronomy 31:9–13).

When Joshua was old and just before he died, he gathered all the leaders and got the word out to the Israelites to remember their story, their lost lines. He exhorted them to "Be very strong; be careful to obey all that is written in the Book of the Law of Moses, without turning aside to the right or to the left. . . . you are to hold fast to the LORD your God, as you have until now" (Joshua 23:6, 8).

Once again, the people began to live a different set of lines with tragic consequences. Rebellion and wars followed, and the kingdom eventually divided. Each was reigned by a series of mostly bad kings. It appeared the lines the people of God were meant to live were truly lost. But God had not abandoned them. God sent a series of special messengers to remind His people about their lost lines.

When the prophets appeared, they spoke clearly about the lost lines. They saw the heart of God and all the amazing things God had planned for His people. And they also saw how the people had traded a flourishing life with God for a set of lines that involved sin and rebellion and selfishness and disobedience and wickedness and evil. And they spoke boldly, fiercely, and clearly to the people about their lost lines. Some heard, understood, and lived out their lost lines. Many others chose not to trade in their old script. Hundreds of years went by.

Then King Josiah discovered the lost Book of the Law. He read it to the people, from the least to the greatest, reminding them once again of their lost lines (2 Chronicles 34:30). After a period of revival, the people once again slipped back into living their old script. Soon, the nation was invaded and taken into exile. More years went by.

When Nehemiah and Ezra rebuilt the walls of Jerusalem, they gathered the people, and Ezra read from the Scriptures, reminding the people of their lost lines, their identity, and their story (Nehemiah 1—10).

When Jesus appeared, He constantly reminded people of their lost lines (more on this later). He insisted that from Moses to the prophets, the central theme that binds all of Scripture was to be found in Him (see John 5:31–47). And that we can find our lost lines only through Him.

The story continued in the Book of Acts and the rest of the New Testament. Peter, Paul, and others spoke boldly about Jesus and encouraged people to find and live their lost lines in Jesus.

The Bible also gives us a glorious glimpse of how our lost lines will end.

When we come to Jesus and discover and live our lost lines, it invades our hearts, renews our minds, transforms our souls, and we get to enjoy a more purposeful, rewarding, and satisfying life. A life in tune with the one God wants each of us to live.

This book has evolved over several years as a journey of reflection of some things stirring in my own soul—it started off as a bunch of scribblings on Post-it Notes and a yellow pad about things I was learning, observing, and sensing the Spirit was stretching in my thinking and growth. I bring it as an offering to see if our communal soul needs to be stirred in ways I think will glorify Jesus and His current work in our midst.

In part 1 of the book, we will go on a search for our lost lines. In part 2, we will discover ways we can find our lost lines, and in part 3, we will learn some things that come up while we are on the journey of living our lost lines.

Truth is, your soul comes equipped with a homing device, pulsating with a signal that aims to direct your life toward *something*. Maybe you have this sense of being unmoored in the sea of change our world constantly goes through. Maybe the current circumstances of your life have rocked your story, and you are looking for a great next chapter. Maybe you perceive a hunger for a world to be birthed anew that is not the world we live in.

Point is,
    this is your one and only life.
    Your lost lines are waiting.
    Start where you are.
    Be open. Be bold. Explore.
    Face your greatest fears.
    Wrestle with the deep questions of life.
    Find and inhabit a story that ignites your soul.

Anyone can find and live their lost lines,
   *but not everyone will.*

I pray
that at the end of this journey, while you'll still be you,
     your heart will be unimaginably transformed by
     Jesus,
that you will discover what it means to walk closely with
     Jesus and soak in His peace and joy and love like
     the very air you breathe,
that you'll start seeing each day, *this day*, as a gift to join
     in the grand adventure of living your lost lines.

Take a deep breath.
   And step forward.

## Part One
# THE SEARCH

# Chapter 1

# GIVEN

You say, "I am rich. I have everything I want. I don't need a thing!" And you don't realize that you are wretched and miserable and poor and blind and naked.

*—Revelation 3:17 NLT*

To be nobody but yourself—in a world which is doing its best, night and day, to make you everybody else—means to fight the hardest battle which any human being can fight; and never stop fighting.

*—e. e. cummings*

A few years ago one summer, I took my two oldest daughters to a local Barnes and Noble. I was passing by the magazines when I stopped at the women's section.

I called out to Elizabeth (who was twelve at the time) and Ashlynne (who was nine) and told them to take a look. I said, "These are the magazines women in our country read. These are some of the most widely circulated magazines in our nation and culture— magazines like *InStyle, Glamour, People, Cosmopolitan, Redbook, Seventeen, Vogue*—and they are read by tens of millions of women each month."

And then I said to them, "According to these magazines, what is the most important thing a woman in America needs to read about this summer? In fact, these topics are so important for women that they are the cover story."

They looked and I looked, and there were stories about which swimsuits make you look the sexiest, the latest fashion trends, summer style guide, how to get a great body before summer, how to flatten your abs by summer, how to get amazing skin this summer, age-defying secrets, and so on.

So I asked to see if we could find a woman's magazine that talked about how to build great character, how to find purpose and significance in our lives, how to think deep thoughts, and so on. We sifted through the rack, and after just two minutes, we found that there were none.

As we moved to the café area and sat down, I told my daughters, "One day, you will grow up and leave home. As disheartening as that is to think of right now, the day is coming; you will do that. When you do, you will enter a world that will flood you with these headlines—telling you that your worth comes from how you look. A world that will tell you your greatest accomplishment in any summer is how well you look in a swimsuit.

"You will enter a world where there will be men that look at you a certain way, who will pass comments or say things that will relate only to your outer looks. If I am around, I will take care of them, but when I am not around, you will be left to make those choices on your own. Nobody can force you to base your self-worth one way or the other. It's going to be totally your call. What are you going to base your self-worth on?"

The next few minutes were so rich.

The truth is, in our society, it starts early.

*We are given a certain script.*

In her book *Consuming Kids*, author Susan Linn states that American companies spend $15 billion a year marketing to kids. And in *Born to Buy*, author Juliet Schor reports that before the time American kids reach their second birthday, they can ask for products by brand name. By the time they hit kindergarten, American children can name some two hundred brands, accumulating possessions at a fast clip, with an average of seventy toys a year.

The advent of screens has made the delivery of these messages more pervasive, easier, and persistent. Common Sense Media reported in 2015 that American teens spend an average of nine hours a day using media. The $200 billion dollar American advertising industry knows this fact. According to *Born to Buy*, they spend more than $15 billion a year on shaping our children's identities, wants, and cravings.

I read a report by YWCA, "Beauty at Any Cost," that detailed how the American cosmetic and fashion industry has developed a pervasive narrative designed to make American girls cradle-to-grave consumers. The opening lines in the report said, "Every woman in the United States participates in a daily beauty pageant, whether she likes it or not. Engulfed by a popular culture saturated with images of idealized, air-brushed and unattainable female physical beauty, women and girls cannot escape feeling judged on the basis of their appearance." The report detailed how this leads to a host of problems from eating disorders to millions spent on cosmetic surgeries each year to low self-esteem, bullying, and discrimination against those who look "below average."

And girls and women aren't alone. NPR reports that boys are falling behind in education, GPAs, and graduation rates, and more and more men are falling out of the workplace. The US Department of Labor reports that there are now more women than men working in high-paying management, professional, and related occupations.

There is a new perceived goal of success. *USA Today* reported on a Pew Research poll in 2007 of Americans in their late teens and early twenties that revealed the highest aspiration of young Americans is to get rich (81 percent) and famous (51 percent).

Multiple factors play into the narrative of what it now
    means to be a man like,
the shift in societal expectations of the role of men and
    women,
our culture's relentless drumbeat that tells us our biggest
    ambition should be the pursuit of a safe
    and comfortable and convenient lifestyle,
the rise of soul-sucking habits like video games
    and porn,
the devaluing of marriage and sex,
a general, gradual, steady, relentless lowering of the
    bar of what it really means to be a man.

To reverse-paraphrase the three main points of John
    Eldredge's best-selling book for men, *Wild At
    Heart*, many of our men have
no meaningful battles to fight,
no grand adventures to go on,
no beauties to rescue.
We are safe, we are comfortable, we are bored, we
    are adrift.

If we stop long enough to pay attention, something within us is telling us that this is not the life we were meant to live. These are not the lines we were meant to enact. And unless we find our lost lines, there are plenty of voices and influences and opinions offering us substitutes.

We are living in the greatest advertising ecosystem the world has ever known. In an article on the pervasiveness of advertising, *The New York Times* reported the average American is exposed to thousands of advertising messages a day. A person living in a city could see up to 5,000 messages a day.

An article in *The Atlantic* said Americans spent $70 billion buying lottery tickets in 2014. $70 billion! To give you context, the amount Americans spend on lottery tickets in the forty-three states where the lottery is legal is more than what all fifty states spend on sports tickets, books, video games, movie tickets, and music sales *combined*. It's equal to the GDP of Kenya.

On the social front, we have stopped talking to each other. Many of us get our sense of community via social media. We send billions of texts, tweets, and selfies and make hundreds of friends, but we are lonelier than ever. A *Fortune* article on chronic loneliness by Laura Entis reported that while between 11 and 20 percent of Americans regularly or frequently felt lonely in the 1970s and 1980s, this figure had risen to 40 to 45 percent in 2010.

We no longer tell meaningful tales around the fire over a meal with our family, friends, and neighbors. Our world is filled with mostly shallow stories in 140 characters or less. If we dare to express an opinion, most of the time we do so from behind anonymous screen alter egos. Too often, these are not meant to lift the human soul in any profound way.

Technology inundates every waking moment of our lives. We handle so much information and data that we have no time to think. We seek to find someone who can help us make sense of it in a way that doesn't upset our preconceived and predetermined opinions. We may have access to the truth somewhere in there, but it is buried and lost, and we fear we are so busy with modern life and so distracted with trivialities and so overwhelmed with the constant clamoring noise that we may never find it.

And all these messages, voices, chatter, and buzz are all
	selling us a story—
They are telling us these are the lines you are designed
	to live.
This is how you are expected to look.
This is how you are meant to behave.
This is how you are supposed to act and react.
These are the things you are supposed to own and
	display and maintain.
This is what you need to drink, this is what you need to
	eat, this is what you need to wear.
This is what will give you happiness and joy and
	satisfaction.
This is your life.
This is your destiny.
This is your role.
This is who you were meant to be.
Here is the script of your life—these are your lines.

The messages we receive from multiple channels impact every
aspect of our lives—the kinds of places we choose to live, the
kinds of products we purchase, the way we manage our money,
the way we parent, the way we view marriage and relationships,
the way we think of sexuality, the way we spend our time, the kinds
of activities we choose to engage in. Billions of dollars are being
spent right now to convince us that we ought to do these things a
certain way.

From the time we were young, even before entering
kindergarten, we have been handed a story, a script, a set of lines,
and told that this is what life is and this is who you are.

And maybe, just maybe, some of us have never questioned
whether it is the right narrative, whether we are speaking the right

lines and living the right story and playing the right part with this unique and awesome gift of our one and only lives.

And the words of the Apostle Paul ring out like a clarion call slicing through the noise, the chatter, the buzz, the hype:

> Do not conform to the pattern of this world, but be transformed by the renewing of your mind. Then you will be able to test and approve what God's will is—his good, pleasing and perfect will.
>
> —*Romans 12:2*

We will return to Romans 12:2 again and again because what Paul said two thousand years ago is just as relevant today.

Paul is saying there is a script the world will hand you and convince you it's who you are.

Don't conform to that lie.

Don't follow or obey or adopt those lines.

*Because that's not your story.*

# Chapter 2

# ACHE

My heart aches with longing.
—*Psalm 119:20 GNT*

There is no agony like bearing an untold story inside you.
—*Zora Neale Hurston*, Dust Tracks on the Road

Some time back, I was meeting with two colleagues at work and we were talking about some things when, and I don't quite know how the conversation went this way, we started toying with this question—who are the top ten people living in our world now you would love to meet?

As I was thinking about this, I mentioned Melinda Gates. I find her to be one of the smartest, most articulate thinkers and difference makers in our world. She's married to some guy named Bill(!) and together they are worth tens of billions of dollars. According to *Business Insider*, they are the richest couple in the world, and she is the richest woman in the world.

Now let's think about this for a moment—if you are the richest person in the world, what would you do? Would you travel the world, live in ultimate luxury, buy the biggest yacht there is, live in the Cinderella castle in Disneyworld? What would you do if you were the richest person in the world?

Melinda Gates used to be a high-powered business executive. Now she heads a foundation with her husband that is committed to world health and education. One of the many things she is passionate about is ending polio, which as recently as 1988 affected hundreds of thousands of children, paralyzing them for life. So she travels to some of the poorest and most desperate slums of India. She meets with local people, spearheading the polio initiative.

In 2010, CBS ran a program on her on *60 Minutes*, which I watched. She shuns publicity, and the CBS team had to ask repeatedly for more than a year before she agreed to have them come along. In the *60 Minutes* program, you see the joy in her face as she walks past sewers and a densely populated area of a slum outside Mumbai. You see her walk into a shanty, you see her joining local teams and administrating the two drops of polio vaccine to a child, and you see her talk passionately about the goal and strategy for ending polio. And while I was watching the program, the thought that came to my mind was this:

*Why would one of the world's richest women leave safety, security, comfort, and convenience and spend her time in the slums of India?*

Why is she walking in the filth and squalor of what many people would term discarded humanity?

Why would anyone with *that* kind of wealth engage in *this* kind of work?

These are very important questions.

We live in a world full of tasks and noise and distractions. For some people at least, life is hectic, a ten-hour work day, dead-end job, a crazy schedule or work to maintain a lifestyle, a life focused on the self. So many of us are frazzled and overwhelmed, and a term I often hear when I ask people how are they doing—crazy busy.

And yet, there is this gnawing in our soul that tells us something is not right. That the lines we are living are not the lines we were meant to live. And it leaves many people disillusioned, bewildered, and lost.

While the glittering promises of the lines this world tries to hand us seem alluring, they do not teach us

> how to live a meaningful life,
> how to form deep relationships,
> how to steward our gifts,
> how to leave a legacy,
> how to find our true north,
> how to cope with loss,
> how to overcome failure and rise from the ashes,
> how to battle greed, addiction, sin, shame, and guilt,
> how to experience true joy, real love, and lasting peace,
> how to save ourselves.

Author Gail Sheehy, in her book *New Passages*, recounts one interview with a young Generation X woman who said, "We are searching for a conscience. We believe there is more to life than the warped world we live in."

This gnawing, this aching, this yearning is universal. And I believe a lot of people in a rich nation like ours, including many Christians, feel this way. That somehow the lines we are speaking and living do not resonate fully with our souls.

Something is amiss. There's got to be something more to life. Those that never take the time to listen to this gnawing and ache of their soul or never find what their soul is looking for can end up in a state of low-grade despair.

Danish philosopher, Søren Kierkegaard wrote:

**We are all like smooth pebbles thrown so as to skim and dance over the surface of the water. But we feel ourselves running out of momentum, and we fear that the inevitable moment is coming when there will be nothing left but to sink into a hundred thousand fathoms of nothingness.**

One hundred thousand fathoms of nothingness. Sounds very similar to the words of a man of tremendous intellect, wealth, and power. King Solomon wrote these words three thousand years ago:

> "Meaningless! Meaningless!" says the Teacher. "Utterly meaningless! Everything is meaningless."
>
> —*Ecclesiastes 1:2*

We all come equipped with a low frequency signal that is being emitted from the recesses of our soul. It is something deep, something primal, something innate and intense and profound. It gnaws at us and calls us to live our lost lines. This signal often gets drowned by the loud buzz and hype and noise of our world, but it refuses to go away. And if we were to stop long enough to listen carefully, we can discover the path to our lost lines. Our souls ache for this.

Writing in his book, *Mere Christianity*, C. S. Lewis puts it this way:

> **If I find in myself a desire which no experience in this world can satisfy, the most probable explanation is that I was made for another world.**

If you look at people who are making a difference, there is the moment in their lives when something changed. It impacted their worldview, their priorities, their life choices. It starts at that pivotal moment when they stop long enough to listen to this gnawing of the soul.

I believe it happened for Melinda Gates one day, and I believe it happened for Zacchaeus.

Luke 19:1–10 tells Zacchaeus's story: "He [meaning Jesus] entered Jericho and was passing through" (Luke 19:1 ESV).

So one day, Jesus comes to the town of Jericho. He is passing through on His way to Jerusalem where He will be crucified for our sins. Jericho was a very wealthy city. And Jesus is passing through this city and there is a crowd following Him. "And behold, there was a man named Zacchaeus. He was a chief tax collector and was rich" (v. 2 ESV).

Now the way tax was collected in those days is that the Romans farmed out the job. They would choose a city or district and then sell the right to tax to the highest bidder. And the highest bidder would then collect all the taxes he could and keep everything beyond what he had to give to the Romans. It was a system of political oppression combined with economic injustice designed to get maximum revenue.

So you can imagine how deeply the tax collectors were hated. They were considered traitors of Israel. They were considered unclean and were not allowed to enter synagogues.

And Zacchaeus is called a chief tax collector. In other words, he had other tax collectors working for him. And he worked in Jericho, a wealthy city.

So here is this man, with lots of power and status, deeply despised, very rich, and he hears Jesus is in town.

And he was seeking to see who Jesus was, but on account of the crowd he could not, because he was small in stature. So he ran on ahead and climbed up into a sycamore tree to see him, for he was about to pass that way.

—vv. 3–4 ESV

Why?

Why was Zacchaeus so eager to see Jesus?

Why did he run? People in that culture, especially men who had wealth and titles, did not run. He runs. He is very eager to see Jesus.

Why?

The Bible doesn't tell us explicitly, but I think one possible reason was this—Zacchaeus has spent his life conforming to a set of lines and playing a part. He's got a big house, he's got a good job, and he's got plenty of money and possessions.

But there comes a day when he reckons with the low frequency ache of his soul. It is something deep, something primal, something innate and intense and profound. It gnaws at Zacchaeus and calls him to live his lost lines. He cannot shake it off. And if Zacchaeus were to stop long enough to listen carefully, he would discover the path to his lost lines. Zacchaeus aches for this, even if he doesn't fully understand what it is he is aching for.

But he hears that Jesus is in town. He has likely heard how Jesus is not like the other religious leaders. There is a guy in his inner circle who also happens to be a tax collector. This captivates him. Maybe Jesus has the answer to this ache of his soul. And so here he is up a sycamore tree, which has low branches and thick foliage, perfect for a short man wanting to hide and watch Jesus pass by.

And something remarkable happens. He can see Jesus. He can see the crowd. They come toward the tree where he is hiding. Closer and closer they come. And now Jesus is right under the tree, and He stops!

And when Jesus came to the place, he looked up and said to him, "Zacchaeus, hurry and come down, for I must stay at your house today" (v. 5 ESV).

Zacchaeus is ecstatic. He throws a lavish dinner party for Jesus. This is probably the first big party Zacchaeus has had in his house.

No one wants to mix with a tax collector. He is thrilled. He lays out a feast, a banquet. And then he says this:

> "Behold, Lord, the half of my goods I give to the poor. And if I have defrauded anyone of anything, I restore it fourfold." And Jesus said to him, "Today salvation has come to this house, since he also is a son of Abraham. For the Son of Man came to seek and to save the lost."
>
> —vv. 8–9 ESV

Zacchaeus is now a son of Abraham. He is now part of the community of God, not because of genealogy, but because of Jesus. Jesus then explains the story of Zacchaeus as part of His greater mission to seek and save the lost.

That low frequency signal of our soul is designed to lead us to Jesus. Because when you come to Jesus, He not only forgives you, He transforms you, He changes you. You become a new creation, a new person, the old has gone, the new has come. You get to ditch the old script and get your lost lines.

Following Jesus as Lord means you understand, as Zacchaeus understood, you were not given all that grace and forgiveness and love and peace and joy just for yourself. It's not just about you. You are now living the script that you were created to live (more on this later).

In 2010, Melinda Gates gave a TED Talk about what nonprofits can learn from Coca-Cola, which I think is one of the best presentations I have ever seen. If you work in the nonprofit sector, you need to see this talk with your team—it will change the way you think of strategy. She ended her talk by hypothesizing if Coca-Cola marketers came to her and asked her to define happiness, she, one of the richest women in the world, would answer that it would be a woman holding her healthy baby. That is her deep happiness.

At the deepest level of our souls, we know we are not on this planet just for their own selves. That somehow one of life's greatest sources of satisfaction comes from serving others and helping others, especially those who are less fortunate than us. That our lost lines do not revolve around us alone. It calls us to live a life of growth and flourishing and maturity and impact that goes way beyond ourselves.

And we are all aching for our lost lines, even if we do not know that is what we are yearning for.

# Chapter 3

# DISCONNECT

For what our human nature wants is opposed to what the spirit wants, and what the spirit wants is opposed to what our human nature wants.
—*Galatians 5:17 GNT*

In a real sense everything that we see is a shadow cast by that which we do not see. . . . All of our new knowledge, all of our new developments, cannot diminish his being one iota. These new advances have banished God neither from the microcosmic compass of the atom nor from the vast, unfathomable ranges of interstellar space. The more we learn about this universe, the more mysterious and awesome it becomes. God is still here.
—*Martin Luther King Jr.*, The Measure of a Man

Let's start with a mini self-assessment, shall we? Think back to the last time you were at a church service. Relive that service for a moment. Whatever else was going on in your life, you felt that was the place to be. You went believing some things and perhaps expecting certain things—that you would worship God, would be with a community of God, and would hear a word from God.

You drove up. You parked your car. You walked to the door and entered in. You were greeted, perhaps handed a bulletin, and you made your way to a seat. You participated in worship, you heard what was going on in the church community, you heard the Word of God being preached, you prayed, and you greeted your friends.

Now, take a look at the line below. It's a line that shows a progressive awareness of being close to God. Here's what I want you to do. Put an S on the scale signifying how close you felt to God when you were imagining yourself at that church service. Did you feel very close to God at church, worshipping and listening to the Word? Somewhat close to God? Not that close to God? Not at all close to God? Go ahead and put an S on the scale (The S signifies Sunday or time at a church service).

| NOT AT ALL CLOSE TO GOD | NOT THAT CLOSE TO GOD | SOMEWHAT CLOSE TO GOD | VERY CLOSE TO GOD |

Now, think back this last week. Let your mind travel to Monday and Tuesday or another weekday. How close did you feel to God during your commute, at work, at school, doing chores, at the grocery store? To help you discern this, I'm going to describe someone who is living in awareness of God's presence and someone who is not.

Someone who is living in awareness of God's presence experiences the peace of God. They have an inner joy, built from conversation with God in prayer and time in the Word. Though this person may be busy, they are not hurried or rushed.

Someone who is not living in recognition of God's presence will be rushed, discontent, worried, engaged in gossip, isolated, angry, bitter, guilty, shameful, lustful, selfish, you get the idea.

So how close did you feel you were to God on the weekdays this last week? If you have had both high and low moments, just average it out and put a W on the scale to signify how close you felt to God on Monday and weekdays.

Is there a gap between the S and the W? When I did this quiz at my church during a church service, hundreds of folks admitted (including yours truly) that there is at least a tiny little gap between my S and my W. For some of us, that gap might actually be quite big.

This is a problem, isn't it?

There seems to be a disconnect.

Even among serious disciples of Jesus.

On what we know to be true on Sunday and what we experience on weekdays.

You may be thinking . . . *On Sundays, I am in church, so of course, I feel close to God. But on Monday, I am not in church. On Monday last week, I was working in a tough job environment, I had a disagreement with my spouse, I was running multiple errands, I had an emergency, I hit a crisis, I had an accident, I fell sick, I gave in to sin, I yelled at my kids for fighting, I burnt the dinner.*

> Which, of course, raises a whole bunch of questions—
> If we feel close to God at church on Sunday, where is the
>     church on Monday?
> Does the church cease to exist from Monday to
>     Saturday?
> If we feel close to God on Sunday and not on Monday,
>     does that mean God is less relational and less
>     present on Mondays?

Or you might be thinking, *I feel close to God when I worship and sing praise songs. I don't do that on Mondays, so I feel less close to God.*

Which raises a whole bunch of other questions—
What exactly is worship?
Is it just singing worship songs?
Is it when we stand and engage in corporate praise?
Is it the time we set aside at the beginning of each
    service?
Is that all there is to worship?

Which actually raises a whole bunch of other questions—
Is the presence of God fleeting?
Is it sporadic?
Is it available only at designated spaces, or is God truly
    omnipresent?
Is God close to us during certain parts of the week and
    then checked out during other parts of the week?
Is church and Christianity and our walk with Jesus and
    the way of Jesus simply this—what happens on
    Sundays stays on Sundays?
But then Monday (ugh!) comes around!

One of the first things I learned when I arrived in the United States more than twenty years ago is that we have this acronym we get very excited about—TGIF. Thank God it's Friday! It's always said with that exclamation mark at the end.

What if we asked someone from another time and another culture to look in at us and write a report about this from the viewpoint of a cultural anthropologist? What would that look like? Here's my feeble attempt at it:

A report on the People of the American Culture
(Examining their attitudes and behaviors on certain days of the week)
Circa 2018

*A majority of people either hates or feels completely disengaged from what they do during the week to earn a living. But it appears that a lot of people in this culture get really excited about one particular day of the week. It's like the old story of the Israelites making bricks for the Pharaoh. Day in day out—bricks, more bricks, extra bricks. They did not have any days off, but people in this culture do.*

*Fridays are especially auspicious. Americans in this time period generally get up on Fridays with a smile because after having slaved away for five days making bricks, and they know 5:00 p.m. is only eight hours away. At the workplace, one notices there is less anger, more tolerance, less grumbling, and more pleasantries on Fridays. The morning goes by smoothly enough, and some of the workers mentally check out around lunch. And then the hour of freedom comes. The clock strikes 5:00, and escape is within reach.*

*As people file out of work, one can tell that this is a moment of great joy because the whole weekend is ahead. Some are packing for a trip. Newspapers and magazines have articles with big headlines on how to escape for the weekend (because there is no escape during the week).*

*Some employers have pity on their employees and require less bricks to be made on Fridays so people can take off a little early. Other employers join in the celebration by making Friday "casual." Productivity at work slumps on Fridays (less bricks are made on Fridays than any other day), and social media interaction picks up dramatically (the two may be related).*

*There are also many songs written about this great day that celebrate its promise of bringing happiness to everyone.*

*Fridays also bring joy because it is most often also pay day. So it is no surprise that Fridays are the biggest day for shopping (with a special Friday called Black Friday being the biggest shopping day of the year). After work, some head for the weekly ritual of eating out. There's even a national restaurant chain called TGI Fridays. In fact, Americans spend more money eating out than on groceries. A family of four spends an average of nearly $10,000 in restaurants each year.*

*Clearly, there is a sense that even God loves Fridays.*

*Mondays are another story.*

*Right around Sunday evening, a general sense of dread takes over the masses. And when Monday morning rolls around, no one says TGIM.*

*People are grumpy, discontent, short-tempered, and sad.*

*There are many songs written about Monday as well, but these are mostly sad songs.*

*And then Tuesday comes and hope springs like a tiny little plant breaking through a crack in the asphalt. By Wednesday and Thursday, the plant of hope grows into a shrub, then a bush. And by Friday, the whole cycle is repeated again.*

TGIF! Yay!

TGIM? Hmmm. Not so much.

I have never heard anyone say TGIM—Thank God it's Monday. But isn't the Lord of Sunday also the Lord of Monday? If we believe this to be true, then we must wrestle with this conundrum if we are to find our lost lines.

Psychologists call this cognitive dissonance, which is a term given to someone whose beliefs and actions don't match up.

Cognitive dissonance happens when there is incongruence between our beliefs and behaviors, between our values and actions. We often work hard to remove or eliminate the dissonance. Imagine a seesaw in a playground. On one side of the seesaw sits our values and beliefs, and on the other side sits our behaviors and actions. We experience peace of mind when the seesaw is in balance, when our beliefs and behaviors are in harmony, when we are actually practicing what we believe. But if our beliefs and behaviors are not in sync, we experience dissonance. And we do all we can to put the seesaw back into balance.

If you believe something to be true but you act in ways that are inconsistent with your beliefs, then you will either change your beliefs or you will change your behavior. You will not want to remain in imbalance for too long.

Consider the speed limit. Let's say it is fifty-five miles per hour. But you routinely drive faster than the speed limit. You know the law, and you know you are doing something wrong. Your belief that you shouldn't be driving at that speed is in violation with your behavior. The seesaw is out of balance.

You will work to bring it into balance. You will either slow down (change your behavior to match your belief) or you will make all sorts of mental excuses as to why speeding in your case is justified (change your belief to match your behavior).

No one drives at 55 mph on this road anyway.
I have an appointment that's too important to miss.
I am a very experienced driver.
Law enforcement officers do not give tickets to people
going ten miles over the speed limit, so it is OK.
I am late for church!

You will work to bring the seesaw into balance.

There are lots of examples of this in the Bible. Jonah comes to mind. Here's how his story begins:

> The word of the LORD came to Jonah son of Amittai: "Go to the great city of Nineveh and preach against it, because its wickedness has come up before me." But Jonah ran away from the LORD and headed for Tarshish. He went down to Joppa, where he found a ship bound for that port. After paying the fare, he went aboard and sailed for Tarshish to flee from the LORD.
>
> —*Jonah 1:1–2*

He knows what he should do, but his actions are in complete imbalance with his beliefs and values. He ends up literally in a dark place. (It must have been dark in the belly of the fish!) The only way out is to get the seesaw back into balance—get his actions to line up with his beliefs and convictions.

Our Romans 12:2 passage reminds us that we cannot conform to the world (live our given lines) and be transformed (live our lost lines) both at the same time. If we do, we will live with this sense of disconnect. We will constantly experience a spiritual cognitive dissonance. Because in and through Christ, there is a complete transformation, a total makeover from the inside out. The seesaw is in balance for the true follower of Jesus. Our actions and behaviors match our beliefs and values.

Of course, when we sin, stumble, and fall prey to the lure of the old lines, God is always there to forgive us and restore us if we come to Him and confess and repent of our sins. Which is exactly what Jonah does. He turns to God and is restored. God, of course, is present right in the middle of our disconnect and spiritual cognitive dissonance.

From inside the fish Jonah prayed to the Lord his God. He said: "In my distress I called to the Lord, and he answered me. From deep in the realm of the dead I called for help, and you listened to my cry. . . . To the roots of the mountains I sank down; the earth beneath barred me in forever. But you, Lord my God, brought my life up from the pit. . . . When my life was ebbing away, I remembered you, Lord, and my prayer rose to you, to your holy temple." . . . And the Lord commanded the fish, and it vomited Jonah onto dry land.

*—Jonah 2:1–10*

I was installing a new filter in our refrigerator the other day. The instructions said I needed to flush the filter with four gallons of water before drinking any water. So I put the filter in, pressed a glass on the water dispenser, and within moments I had a glass filled with white foamy water. I wanted to drink a clean glass of water. Would it help if I simply added clean water to the dirty water? Or what if I dumped the water, but did not wash the glass and filled it with clean water? Neither of these would work. I had to drain four gallons of water, throw all the dirty water out, clean the glass, and then pour myself a clean glass of water.

Trying to live a life of transformation in Christ while keeping certain parts of life out of reach of our Lord is like trying to add clean water into a glass that already has some dirty foamy water in it. It doesn't work.

If we are to receive and understand and live our lost lines, we must identify and dismantle and remove this disconnect (the conforming, the dirty water) from our lives and bring every aspect of our lives under the lordship of Christ (the transforming, the clean water). We will have to root out spiritual cognitive dissonance from our lives. We will need to wrestle with the question of how to close the gap between the S and the W on our chart. Part of it has to do with the masks we wear.

# Chapter 4

# MASKS

You were taught, with regard to your former way of life, to put off your old self, which is being corrupted by its deceitful desires; to be made new in the attitude of your minds; and to put on the new self, created to be like God in true righteousness and holiness.

—*Ephesians 4:22–24*

No man, for any considerable period, can wear one face to himself, and another to the multitude, without finally getting bewildered as to which may be the true.

—*Nathaniel Hawthorne,* The Scarlet Letter

ark Twain, writing in the voice of Huckleberry Finn in *Adventures of Huckleberry Finn,* penned these famous words:

**It made me shiver. And I about made up my mind to pray; and see if I couldn't try to quit being the kind of a boy I was, and be better. So I kneeled down. But the words wouldn't come. Why wouldn't they? . . . I knowed very well why they wouldn't come. . . . It was because I was playing double. I was letting on to give up sin, but way inside of me I was holding on to the biggest one of**

**all. I was trying to make my mouth say I would do the right thing and the clean thing . . . but deep down in me I knowed it was a lie—and He knowed it.**

We chuckle at this, and yet we know it is true! Huckleberry the person was different from Huckleberry the persona he was projecting out to others.

The origin of the word *persona* is interesting. It originates from Latin and means "mask, character played by an actor," signifying the mask actors wore in Roman and Greek theater productions to differentiate between characters.

Everyone knew the characters being portrayed through the *persona* of the actors weren't real. It was all a well-orchestrated part in a play. The actors through the *persona* of their assumed characters in a play were speaking and acting lines they were given. The lines were meant to go with the *persona* they had meticulously memorized, painstakingly put on, and thoughtfully staged.

The person and persona were two distinct things. Imagine an actor from that period refusing to take off the mask but wearing it constantly. Depending upon the occasion and whether he was at work, at home, or at play, he switched between masks to suit the occasion. He never took them off. We would laugh at such a person for being so silly. Everyone can see what is happening.

And yet, aren't some of us doing the same thing?

We try to match the *persona*, or the mask, with the lines we are trying to live. Inside, we know there is a big difference between what we portray and who we really are.

Companies, celebrities, and sports stars spend billions of dollars maintaining the image they want people to think represents who they are, which is not wrong in itself. If you are trying to live your deepest held convictions and values in an authentic way while respecting others, then it is a noble thing. But when we take the concept of branding and apply it to the individual, we can have many unintended consequences.

The concept of personal branding started with the Internet economy. The idea is that every single one of us is just as important a brand as Nike or Apple or Google. Therefore, the thinking goes, we need to think in terms of our biggest selling points, create an online presence that sells our brand, and maintain a highly polished image of who we are supposed to be. The goal is to promote, advance, and market yourself in ways that maximize the rewards. You study what big companies do to grow and maintain their brands, and you transfer those lessons into microsteps for the brand called *You!*

You create an intentional network of people who can help advance your brand. You write carefully crafted op-eds or articles or commentaries in local papers and online that show off your brand. You do what you can to increase visibility.

Historian Daniel Boorstin writes in his book *The Image*, "We risk being the first people in history to have been able to make their illusions so vivid, so persuasive, so 'realistic' that they can live in them."

The result is that we have created a world filled with microstorefronts. Our Facebook page is one display window of our persona. Twitter is another. So is Instagram and Snapchat and YouTube and Pinterest and LinkedIn and dozens of other channels through which we project our persona.

And some of us work very hard to create and advance and maintain the brand we think will best fill our needs and wants. We are walking on the highway of humanity looking at billboards instead of people. In some ways, we are back in a Roman theater watching the personas come out and speak their lines. We get to know the *persona* but have a hard time getting to know the *person*.

All this is hard work and requires an enormous amount of slog and a tremendous amount of energy. One has to constantly think ahead to the next clever post, the next retweet, the next email, the next status update, the next viral cat video. These are all meant to convey a message of who we want others to think we are. Is this why young people sometimes don't want their parents or siblings to connect with them on social media? Their families might see that the person they know at home is so different from the brand, the persona, being projected online.

Interestingly, the word *hypocrite* comes from the Greek word *hypokrites*, which means actor. The word is made up of two Greek words that literally mean "an interpreter from underneath." The person underneath the persona is trying to interpret and act out how they think the mask should behave, speak, and respond.

We are increasingly inhabiting a communal landscape in which we recognize and associate and form relationships with each other on the basis of our projected brands.

> The problem with persona and personal brands is that
> you can never truly be human.
> You cannot be vulnerable.
> You cannot be weak.
> You cannot have a true authentic meaningful relationship
> with a brand.
> Brands are about selling and marketing and projecting,
> not about authenticity and reality and substance
> and being.
>
> The Pharisees had a brand.
> They were serious about God.
> They spent significant time studying the Scriptures.
> They were careful about following the laws.

But, it was primarily a brand, an image, a storefront to
what they wanted people to think.

So Jesus had some things to say about this:
"They do not practice what they preach. . . .
Woe to you, teachers of the law and Pharisees, you
hypocrites!
You shut the door of the kingdom of heaven in people's
faces. . . .
You give a tenth of your spices—mint, dill and cumin.
But you have neglected the more important matters of
the law—justice, mercy and faithfulness. . . .
You clean the outside of the cup and dish, but inside
they are full of greed and self-indulgence. . . .
You are like whitewashed tombs, which look beautiful on
the outside but on the inside are full of the bones
of the dead and everything unclean" (excerpts from
Matthew 23:3–27).

The Pharisees had a carefully cultivated persona. Anybody reading
their Facebook pages and tweets or watching their YouTube
channels would have been suitably impressed. Their clothing,
speech, rituals, and public display all projected a persona. But it was
wildly different from the persons wearing them.

And Paul says to not conform to that. Because all the messages
and chatter and hype will want to conform you into *something you
were never meant to be.* The word *conform* means to give the same
shape, outline, or contour to. It means putting on the shape of a
disguise—to put on the form, fashion, or appearance of another.
And the reason why Paul includes this directive in a letter to a
church is that sometimes taking on a persona can happen *inside a
church.* People can start to live and act and speak in ways that are

not authentic or real, but are the outcome of a person wearing a mask, desiring to create an impression on others. And it can be an extremely dangerous way to live.

Even the early church struggled with matching their person to their persona:

> But a man named Ananias, with his wife Sapphira, sold a piece of property, and with his wife's knowledge he kept back for himself some of the proceeds and brought only a part of it and laid it at the apostles' feet.
>
> —*Acts 5:1–2 ESV*

At first glance, this passage reads like a story of a devoted couple. The couple had a piece of property. They decided to sell it, keep part of the proceeds, and bring the rest to the church. This action would be commendable in a lot of circumstances, but not in this situation.

Peter confronted him, "Ananias, why has Satan filled your heart to lie to the Holy Spirit and to keep back for yourself part of the proceeds of the land?" (v. 3 ESV). And Ananias fell down and died.

To understand what just happened, we need to look at the way this chapter starts. It starts with the word "But," which means it is a continuation of the story in Acts 4. So let's flip back and look at the context.

Acts 4 paints a fascinating picture of the early church. All the believers were of one heart and mind. There was unity in the church. People genuinely cared about each other. They loved each other to the point that no one claimed ownership over their stuff. The love, unity, and generosity of the people meant that the church was firing on all cylinders. The gospel was being preached with boldness, the needs of the poor and the destitute were being met, all the ministries of the church were funded, lives were being transformed, hearts were being changed, people were bringing people to meet Jesus, disciples were making disciples, and people were giving generously, serving faithfully, and worshipping joyfully. People were discovering their lost lines and living them purposefully and enthusiastically and diligently.

People would look at the church and be dazzled by its beauty and potential. And what's more, some members of the church loved God and loved people so much they caught the vision of what the church was and what it could be, and they sold off land or houses they owned and brought the money to the feet of the apostles. And the funds got distributed to those in need.

Luke then tells us the story of one such member. His name was Joseph, and he was from Cyprus and owned a field. Joseph sold it, took the money, and brought it as an offering and laid it down at the apostles' feet. The leaders of the early church gave him a new name. They call him Barnabas, which means "son of encouragement" (v. 36). His new name went with the new lines of his life. He would go on to be a leader in the church who brought people together and spoke words of life and encouragement everywhere he went.

That's how Acts 4 ends, and then we get to chapter 5 and, in the ESV, it starts with "but"—which means the story takes a different turn. There was a couple who attended church, and they saw how it was flourishing and how people like Joseph were being commended and getting new names. Instead of joining in the vision and the calling, they turned inward. They wanted to be seen and perceived as Barnabas was, except they really did not want to be like him. They did not really want to sell their property and give it all to the church. They only wanted the recognition of it.

So they put on a mask. They went through this elaborate charade and sold some real estate and then colluded together to keep back some of the money and give just enough to make an impression in front of the church. They didn't want to grow spiritually. They didn't want to make the sacrifice. They didn't want to be servants of the Lord. They just wanted to be known and attempted to create the impression and perception of spiritual growth, sacrifice, and servanthood.

There is an element of elaborate planning and scheming (see verses 2 and 9). They agreed together that they were going to deliberately wear the mask of spirituality and try to fool the church.

*Except it wasn't just the church they were trying to deceive, was it?*

Peter clarified their source of deception. Let's look again at verse 3. He said, "Ananias, why has Satan filled your heart to lie to the Holy Spirit and to keep back for yourself part of the proceeds of the land?"

The temptation for Ananias and Sapphira to wear a mask of false generosity and spirituality originated from Satan. We have an enemy who would love to keep us from living out our true lines. And then Peter said Ananias was not just trying to deceive the people in the church, *but by lying to the church, he was lying to the Holy Spirit!*

Wearing a mask might deceive some people some of the time, but it will never deceive the Holy Spirit. And when someone starts doing this inside the church, it can have chilling consequences.

We all feel the pull toward the mask, but the mask will get us to spew lines we were never meant to live and own and speak.

It will keep us from finding and living our lost lines.

It will promise great gain without much pain.

The mask will pull us toward deceit and duplicity and death to the true self.

And Paul tells us not to conform to the masks of this world.

If we are to discover our lost lines, we have to start here. To perceive and understand and identify the lines already in place for us and in us and how they disguise the person we were created to be.

In other words, the confession against conformity to the world must precede the transformation by the renewing of our minds our lost lines can bring into our lives.

Jesus talked about this a lot.

> By this time the crowd, unwieldy and stepping on each other's toes, numbered into the thousands. But Jesus' primary concern was his disciples. He said to them, "Watch yourselves carefully so you don't get contaminated with Pharisee yeast, Pharisee phoniness. You can't keep your true self hidden forever; before long you'll be exposed. You can't hide behind a religious mask forever; sooner or later the mask will slip and your true face will be known. You can't whisper one thing in private and preach the opposite in public; the day's coming when those whispers will be repeated all over town.
>
> *—Luke 12:1–3 The Message*

Paul put it this way:

> We refuse to wear masks and play games. We don't maneuver and manipulate behind the scenes. And we don't twist God's Word to suit ourselves. Rather, we keep everything we do and say out in the open, the whole truth on display, so that those who want to can see and judge for themselves in the presence of God.
>
> *—2 Corinthians 4:2 The Message*

We read Paul's words and see the beauty of that. We understand the logic of what he is saying and our hearts crave the authenticity of what he means.

> When we become discerning enough to understand the
> lines our world tries to impress upon us,
> When we understand and reject the idea and practice of
> living in spiritual cognitive dissonance,
> When we become brave enough to start taking our
> masks off,
> We become ready to tune in and receive our lost lines.

# Chapter 5

# TUNING IN

You make known to me the path of life; you will fill me with joy in your presence, with eternal pleasures at your right hand.

—*Psalm 16:11*

I often think: "A life is like a day; it goes by so fast. If I am so careless with my days, how can I be careful with my life?"

—*Henri Nouwen,* The Road to Daybreak

To understand how we can tune in to God and His Spirit and receive our lost lines for the day, I will first need to talk about the American commute, then a little bit about Mary of Nazareth, then the daily news feed you have programmed into your smartphone, then a little more about Mary.

Here we go—starting with the American commute.

In an article helpfully titled, "The American commute is worse today than it's ever been," *The Washington Post* reported the average American commute has risen to an all-time high of 26.4 minutes in 2015. That's approximately 220 hours on the road each year. The article points to America's decades-long suburban sprawl shift as a contributor to the increase in commuting time. The author cites research that shows long commute times are linked to obesity, high cholesterol, high blood pressure, back and neck pain, divorce, depression, and even death (whew!).

I live in the DC Metro area, which according to the Census Bureau, has the second-longest commute in the country after East Stroudsburg, PA. (What's going on with the people in East Stroudsburg? I am curious, but I guess that's a story for another time.)

The average commute for many of us who live in the DC Metro area is about thirty-two minutes each way—more than an hour every single workday. I was recently stuck in rush-hour traffic, which was extra congested due to an accident, when I happened to look around and see the faces of drivers around me. They looked absolutely miserable. One man was yelling into his phone. Another woman had her hand on her forehead. There were a lot of frowns. A guy kept thumping his steering wheel. I sensed anger, impatience, frustration, and weariness. No one was smiling. No one was happy. No one looked optimistic, upbeat, delighted, or happy.

> And I was thinking, this is reality for a lot of us.
> Commuting, driving around, stuck in traffic, waiting,
> > more waiting, still more waiting.
> Frowns,
> Frustrations,
> Anger,
> Weariness.
>
> If God came into this world as my Savior and Lord, why
> > am I still stuck in traffic?
> Why are things so hard?
> Why do I have to make this tough journey?
> Why did I have to go through that?

> Why can't life get a little more convenient and comfy and calm?
>
> Where is God in all this?

Now then, a little bit about Mary.

She grew up in a little-known town as a little-known teenager. One day, an angel appeared and gave her the startling news that she had been chosen by God to give birth to a Son and that He would be no ordinary baby. He would be the Son of God Most High, the Messiah the people had been waiting for. He would be the King of Israel, and His rule would never end.

Interestingly, things didn't get easy or convenient or comfy or calm for Mary. In fact, toward the end of her pregnancy, she had to make a weeklong commute from Nazareth to Bethlehem. We wouldn't blame Mary if she had thought:

*This is not what I had in mind when I agreed to carry the Messiah in my womb.*

*Why am I not in a palace giving birth to the future King?*

*Why can't I at least have my family and friends near me during this time?*

*If this is God's grand plan, why am I stuck in this difficult commute?*

And then, as Joseph and Mary took another turn in the long and tiring road, maybe she felt the baby move inside her.

*God is here with me in this commute!*

Moving right along, let's talk about news feed.

Millions of us subscribe to customized news feeds. We can tailor the news and chatter that come our way to line up with our views, values, opinions, and biases. We don't have the time to live three-dimensional lives; we would rather have the information chopped up, flattened, and made easily digestible.

In the article, "Your Facts or Mine?" for *The New York Times*, journalist Emma Roller writes, "The strongest bias in American politics . . . is a confirmation bias, or the urge to believe only things that confirm what you already believe to be true. . . . We tend to seek out and remember information that reaffirms what we already believe."

What is this doing to us—individually, as a community, and as a nation? Is it making us into a more united, hopeful, peaceful, loving nation where intelligent and respectful dialogue can take place?

Or is it making us suspicious of others who think and vote and live differently from the way we do, making us doubtful, divisive, and distrustful, and shutting down any hope of a dialogue with those who have opposing views?

Cynicism is the dominant current mood in our culture and our world. We don't want to trust anyone who is outside our desired and stated "group." We fear being let down. We worry about being deceived. We don't want to get hurt again. So we close the walls around us and try our best to protect ourselves from "them." Meanwhile "they" are doing the same thing.

Conformity to the things of this world, the circumstances of this life, the hype and chatter of our world, buying into the cynicism of our day, the lines our world hands us will eventually suck the hope and the joy out of us. It will make us cynical, distrustful, and suspicious. It will convince us that there is no use trying. Things are not going to get better. Give up hope.

And one day feels and looks and unfolds like any other.

Author Ann Voskamp writes in her book, *One Thousand Gifts*, "In a world addicted to speed, I blur the moments into one unholy smear."

**What the story of Jesus does,**
**what coming to church on a weekend does,**

what worshipping does,
what listening to a sermon does,
what serving the poor and volunteering at a ministry,
and going on missions,
and joining small groups,
and reading God's Word,
and praying does is it creates these speed bumps along
the way.

Jesus invades the cynicism of our old lines, challenges the hardness of our hearts, and eases the resistance of our minds with the healing news that one day, *this day*, does not have to be like another. Maybe your life and your days right now are one unholy smear. The rush, the speed, the circumstances have been too much. And you believe things are not going to change.

*Unless*
as you take another small turn in a difficult commute,
you realize,
*God is here,*
Immanuel—God with us.

That day, when I was stuck in traffic, the lane next to me suddenly opened up and the cars moved along. *Yes, of course, the other lane gets to go faster.* And then it slowed down again and I saw a car pull up next to me.

And the woman in that car was smiling and singing with all her might to a song playing on her stereo. I couldn't hear a thing, but I couldn't help smiling. *I want to hear what she is hearing.* She was swaying from side to side, and she couldn't have cared less about the traffic, the delay, the inconvenience, because she was tuned into something far greater than her current circumstances.

Bearing Jesus did not make life easy for Mary.
The inconvenience of pregnancy,
the disruption of her schedule,
the upsetting of her plans,

And yet she proclaims:

My soul glorifies the Lord
and my spirit rejoices in God my Savior,
for he has been mindful
of the humble state of his servant.
(Luke 1:46–48)

*Huh?*

Mary is tuned into another channel. A channel that flows the joy and peace and love of God into her soul. She's tuned in. But sometimes we can live our lives not tuning in. And our days end and start in very predictable ways.

So, when you are stuck in traffic, what if you tune into a Christian radio station and make that commute a praise time with God? When the alarm goes off, what if you spent the next five minutes in prayer, in conversation with God at the start of your day, asking Him to open your eyes to what He is up to and join Him in His plan and agenda? What if instead of starting your day with the news feed, you started with a Bible feed?

What will that do to your soul?

What if you allowed God to enter into the most jaded and cynical parts of your heart and you lived every day from this day on with a renewed and greater awareness of God's presence and love and grace all around you?

What if you tuned in?

There'll still be traffic and frustration and delay and inconveniences. But, like Mary, your soul will be singing a new song. Just like the angels and shepherds did on that first Christmas.

In a world of Caesar and Romans and Herod, filled with violence, oppression, brutality, injustice, poverty, slavery, and extreme hardship, the angels insisted they were bringing "good news that will cause great joy for all the people. Today in the town of David a Savior has been born to you; he is the Messiah, the Lord" (Luke 2:10–11).

> A light has appeared in the darkness.
> And people who are stuck in traffic,
> stuck in pain and sorrow,
> stuck in sin and shame,
> stuck in cynicism and fear,
> stuck in oppression and injustice,
> stuck in circumstances and frustrations beyond
>     their control,
> people who are waking each day in anxiety,
> people who are afraid of what they are seeing and
>     hearing is happening in our country and our world,
> people who walk in darkness have seen a great light.

You come to Him and, like Mary, He will give you a new song, He will fill you with His grace, He will flood your heart with His love and hope.

Getting rid of bad lines starts with tuning in and understanding our lost lines.

It's that simple, and it's that hard.

# *Part Two*
# THE FINDING

# Chapter 6

# THE LINE-GIVER

The thief comes only to steal and kill and destroy; I have come that they may have life, and have it to the full.

—*John 10:10*

Jesus does not give recipes that show the way to God as other teachers of religion do. He is himself the way.

—*Theologian Karl Barth*

In the beginning, God created the heavens and the earth. The earth was without form, empty and dark. God then created day and night, land and water, sea creatures and land creatures, birds and vegetation. And everything God created was good. God also made the first man and the first woman. Then:

God blessed them and said to them, "Be fruitful and increase in number; fill the earth and subdue it. Rule over the fish in the sea and the birds in the sky and over every living creature that moves on the ground."

—*Genesis 1:28*

In the beginning of the biblical narrative we are introduced to a God who created the world out of emptiness and darkness in an extravagant display of creative energy and beauty, crafting everything with a purpose and a plan. This is clearly a God whose bent is to bless, a God who meant for His creation to thrive, and a God who delights in the pure goodness of it all.

He created man and woman and gave them the script, the plan, the purpose, for their lives—to take charge, look after, and cultivate the earth under God's loving authority and rule. The text tells us God blessed them and intended them to be a blessing.

Interestingly, all through the creation process God simply speaks and things pop into existence, but when it comes to creating humans, there is a change in style: "God said, '*Let us* make mankind in our image, in our likeness'" (v. 26, emphasis added).

Why the plural? Who is us?

Flip over to John 1, and it says:

> In the beginning was the Word, and the Word was with God, and the Word was God. He was with God in the beginning.
>
> —*John 1:1–2*

The us in Genesis refers to the Father, Son, and Holy Spirit . At the center of who God is, there is this perfect relational community. And so when God says "let us . . . in our image" there is a sense that the relational community of God is now being extended to the creation of man and woman. We were created drastically different from the rest of creation. We were created for some very specific reasons.

The Line-Giver had such grand plans for the first humans, for us. He had these awesome lines for them, for us. But the first humans decide to abandon God's script and adopt their own—one of sin and rebellion.

We see the entry of a dark character into the story. The enemy slithers up to the humans and says, "Did God really say, 'You must not eat from any tree in the garden'?" (Genesis 3:1). We have an enemy, and he wants to keep us from finding and living our lost lines (even after we find them, he works hard to distract us).

He convinced the first humans that abandoning the lines God intended for them (and us) to live was a better way to go. This way, we can then be god of our own lives, making our own choices, and living life the way we want. *We can be like God.*

Except we are not.

As the consequences of living this alternate script unfolded, it fractured the community God had in mind with humans. The lines humans chose broke the relational community between God and them and between each other. You would think the Line-Giver would give up on His creation.

Except He doesn't.

The ache of His heart is still to redeem and restore. He first did this by choosing and building a people who would represent Him and bring His story and blessing and redemption to the rest of the world. He specifically sought out a man named Abraham and revealed His lines to him. Abraham received it and followed his lost lines of being the progenitor of a promised nation through whom all nations of the world would learn their lost lines.

The nation God founded had a sketchy history of mostly ignoring and disobeying God's repeated desire for them to live out their lost lines. Like the first humans, they followed their own lines all the way into slavery. Again, the Line-Giver did not give up on them. He heard their cry for help and rescued them and led them to the Promised Land. The Line-Giver then gave them very specific scripts detailing how they were to be a people set apart, a nation of priests, champions of justice, and caretakers of the poor and oppressed. Perhaps now God's desire for community with His people will be fulfilled.

Except it isn't.

The people chose to follow a script of their own making, with most doing whatever they thought was right in their own eyes. The Line-Giver still did not give up on them but sent a series of prophets who spoke boldly and reminded the people to turn to their lost lines. The prophets were captivated by what following the Line-Giver would look like, and they reminded the people with soaring visions of a life lived following their lost lines.

Once again, the people chose to ignore their lost lines. Their disobedience led to their land being invaded and the nation taken into exile. Throughout the story, a faithful remnant followed their lost lines and looked forward to a time when God's reign would be reestablished and peace and justice would prevail again.

This was fulfilled when the Line-Giver came to earth in the flesh of Jesus, the visible image of the invisible Line-Giver, God. Jesus existed before anything was created and is supreme over all creation, and through Jesus, God created everything in the heavenly realms and on earth. Jesus made the things we can see and the things we can't see—such as thrones, kingdoms, rulers, and authorities in the unseen world. Everything was created through Jesus and for Jesus.

Jesus existed before anything else, and Jesus holds all creation together. Jesus is also the head of the church, which is His body. Jesus is first in everything. For the Line-Giver in all His fullness was pleased to live in Jesus, and through Jesus, the Line-Giver reconciled everything to Himself. He made peace with everything in heaven and on earth by means of Christ's blood on the Cross (Colossians 1:15–20).

And Jesus came bearing the good news that we can now have full access to our lost lines. And to all who received Him, He not only introduced them to their lost lines but gave them the right to be called children of God (John 1:12).

The lines the enemy gave us in Genesis and the lines we have adopted on our own will lead us all the way to death, *eternal death*.

So God made a way in Jesus. Jesus taught us about our lost lines, healing the sick, feeding the hungry, giving sight to the blind, forgiving the sinner, and welcoming the marginalized.

Clearly, through Jesus, the old promise that when we live our lost lines not only are we blessed of God but we become a blessing to others was now becoming a new reality in the kingdom of God, as ushered in by Jesus.

Jesus not only lived and taught us these things, He then died on the Cross as atonement for all the wrong, sinful, shameful lines and scripts we have ever lived, and now all our old lines can be buried at the foot of the Cross. Then He rose from the dead and established His church to remind each generation of their lost lines.

And He longs to call us by our name and be our Lord, our Savior, our Teacher, our Friend, our Line-Giver. He longs to give us our lost lines. To bring love and joy and peace and purpose into our lives and into our world.

And that's not the end of the story—the Bible tells us there is coming a day when all creation will be restored and everything will be the way it was meant to be. On that day:

The wolf will live with the lamb, the leopard will lie down with the goat, the calf and the lion and the yearling together; and a little child will lead them. The cow will feed with the bear, their young will lie down together, and the lion will eat straw like the ox. The infant will play near the cobra's den, and the young child will put its hand into the viper's nest. They will neither harm nor destroy on all my holy mountain, for the earth will be filled with the knowledge of the LORD as the waters cover the sea.

—Isaiah 11:6–9

On that day, when people are perfectly living their lost lines:

> They will beat their swords into plowshares and their spears into pruning hooks. Nation will not take up sword against nation, nor will they train for war anymore.
>
> —*Isaiah 2:4*

On that day:

> God's dwelling place is now among the people, and he will dwell with them. They will be his people, and God himself will be with them and be their God. He will wipe every tear from their eyes. There will be no more death or mourning or crying or pain, for the old order of things has passed away.
>
> —*Revelation 21:3–4*

We will live in a perfect, deep, intimate relational community with each other and with God. Everything and everyone will flourish just as God intended it to back in Genesis.

Our lost lines offer us the chance to choose to live in that future reality right now. The kingdom of God is not fully consummated yet; it is here and it is present and it is expanding in every realm of our world. And when we live out our lost lines we are living our story as part of *that* grand story, a far better story than any other we can find.

> The Line-Giver brings love, joy, hope, and peace like
>     drinks of cool water to the thirsty.
> And because Jesus, the Line-Giver came, and is here,

we can trade our old script for a new script.
We can now have access to our lost lines.

Having been in ministry for more than twenty years, I
　　have seen how this impacts people.
When they understand who this awesome Line-Giver is
　　and what He is offering,
when they receive, understand and live out their lost
　　lines, I have seen,
people who were violent and angry turn into
　　peacemaking, gentle souls,
people who were greedy and selfish become generous
　　and big-hearted,
people who were dishonest and devious turn into people
　　of character and integrity,
people who were proud and pompous become humble
　　servants,
people who hated and hurt others become
　　compassionate and caring,
people who were cynical and bitter turn into tender and
　　loving people,
people who were simply cruising through life get
　　invigorated with passion and purpose.
Finding and living our lost lines will do that.

In a world of opinions shifting by the tide, headlines changing
by the hour, statuses updated by the minute, Scripture tell us in
Hebrews 13:8: Jesus Christ is the same yesterday and today and
forever.

Our Line-Giver does not change.
His message is still the same.

Forgiveness is available.
Grace is accessible.
Receiving our lines from Him is still possible.

Jesus, our Line-Giver is not only fully God and fully man. He is not only our Lord and our Savior. He is our Creator, our Redeemer, our Friend, our Shepherd, and our Guide. He is the wisdom of God, He is the destroyer of old lines and sustainer of those who are trying their best to live their lost lines in a world that can beat anyone down.

He inspires the bored, invites the bypassed, welcomes the forgotten, heals the hurting, restores the sinners, and whispers to those that have wandered away.

He points us to a way of living that is holy and transcendent and adventurous and prompts us—challenges us—to rise above ourselves to become something greater.

And the calling to live our lines with joy and humility and peace and love and passion and gentleness and wisdom and boldness under the extravagant love and direction of the Line-Giver to a script that can transform our lives, our homes, our families, our communities, our countries, our world—if that isn't the greatest mission ever given to humans, then what is?

The Line-Giver is the only One who can renew our minds, transform our lives, and break the shackles of conformity to the old script. And He is ready to give us our lost lines.

How does this happen? It starts with our heart.

A divided heart can never fully live out the lost lines.

But an undivided one reaps the joy of a fulfilled life.

# Chapter 7

# DIVIDED

Their loyalty is divided between God and the world, and they are unstable in everything they do.

*—James 1:8 NLT*

As every divided kingdom falls, so every mind divided . . . confounds and saps itself.

*—Leonardo da Vinci*

Writing two thousand years ago, Roman philosopher Seneca observed in his essay "On the Shortness of Life":

> **It is not that we have a short time to live, but that we waste a lot of it. Life is long enough, and a sufficiently generous amount has been given to us for the highest achievements if it were all well invested. But when it is wasted in heedless luxury and spent on no good activity, we are forced at last by death's final constraint to realize that it has passed away before we knew it was passing. So it is: we are not given a short life but we make it short, and we are not ill-supplied but wasteful of it.**

We live fractured lives. We deeply perceive the siren call of our souls to living our lost lines. But the lives we are living seem to run on a different set of rules, running on a mechanism we are unable to stop or slow down. The dichotomy of our existence stresses us, lulls us, and draws us toward taking the path of least resistance. We drift away from our lost lines. *And whenever we are in drift mode, we are usually not drifting in the right direction.*

Living our lost lines means we will have to rise up against the drift, the pull of the current, and refuse to be dragged downstream by the current of inertia. It will involve sacrifice. It will cost us something. Some will look at the cost and decide the price is too steep. Some will walk part of the way and then walk away. This is why I wrote in the opening pages of this book that anyone can find and live their lost lines, but not everyone will.

Sometimes people come to the Line-Giver, find their lost lines, but still choose to walk away. Because it's not always easy. This is going to cost you something.

There was once a king. His name was Amaziah. His story starts this way:

> Amaziah was twenty-five years old when he became king, and he reigned in Jerusalem twenty-nine years. His mother's name was Jehoaddan; she was from Jerusalem. He did what was right in the eyes of the LORD, but not wholeheartedly.
> —2 Chronicles 25:1–2

*But not wholeheartedly.*
What a startling little fact about a king who aimed to do
    what was right before God.
He came to the Line-Giver.
He understood his lines.
He embraced his role.
Then he drifted.
He just didn't do it wholeheartedly.

Let's go a little deeper into his story.

Amaziah became king after his father Joash was murdered by his own officials. Amaziah's first act was to punish those officials. The prevailing custom was to punish entire families for such crimes, but the text tells us "he executed the officials who had murdered his father the king. Yet he did not put their children to death" (vv. 3–4). He spared the children in accordance with God's laws laid down in Deuteronomy 24. His father had made the teaching of the Law a signature accomplishment of his reign, and Amaziah would have likely been present in many of the gatherings where such teachings took place.

Amaziah started off well. Then things started to change. He began rebuilding the army and soon drafted 300,000 soldiers. A battle was brewing with the Edomites, and Amaziah wanted to make sure he had enough troops. So he hired 100,000 additional mercenaries from outside his kingdom for the sum of 100 talents of silver.

Enter a man of God who tells Amaziah this was a bad move. He should have consulted God. Nevertheless, the man of God tells him to let the 100,000 soldiers go, and God will give Amaziah victory over the Edomites.

Amaziah responded, "But what about the hundred talents I paid for these Israelite troops?" (v. 9).

Amaziah heard clearly from God. He knows exactly what his lost lines are for this day, this moment. But his first reaction is, what about the money? What about the sacrifice? What about the cost? He quickly jumps to doing a cost-benefit analysis of following God.

The man of God assures him, "The LORD can give you much more than that" (v. 9). Amaziah fired the 100,000 soldiers he had hired from outside his kingdom, but only after being assured the benefits of following God's script outweighed the benefits of the script he came up with.

He followed God but not wholeheartedly. Jesus talked about this very thing in Matthew 6:24. He said no one can serve two masters. You cannot live with a divided heart for long. You will end up being devoted to one and despising the other. You cannot inhabit two stories. You will eventually have to choose. And there are consequences to living the wrong script.

Those 100,000 fired soldiers are furious. And they cause a tremendous amount of heartache for a whole lot of people on their rampage back to their homes.

Still, Amaziah's obedience leads to a great victory. But then Amaziah does something inexplicable. While it was customary for victors to plunder the land they had conquered, Amaziah went further. He brought back pagan idols and gods and installed them and worshipped them.

Amaziah went completely off script. You cannot live two scripts. Eventually you have to choose. So in this scene of his life, Amaziah drifted and chose to abandon his lost lines. God, in His mercy, sent a prophet to remind Amaziah of his lost lines. But Amaziah got mad at the prophet! Pride and arrogance now clouded his judgment and he no longer sought after God. He picked a fight with the king of Israel and was soundly defeated. His kingdom was looted. He was left bereft of any power and influence. We don't hear very much about the second half of Amaziah's reign. Nothing remarkable happened. He lived in seclusion and fear. Fifteen years of insignificance until he was assassinated (2 Chronicles 25:27).

You can come to the Line-Giver and find your lost lines, but the choice is still yours. You can still walk away. Amaziah isn't the only example in the Bible of someone turning from his lost lines. One time a rich young guy went to Jesus. All the wealth and status and comfort did not satisfy his soul, so he went to Jesus. Jesus gave him his lost lines. And the young man looked at his lines and said, "No, I think I am going to do this on my own. I will live my own story. I am going to follow the script of this world." (See Matthew 19:16–22.)

That is a sad story, but one people still follow. I have seen it happen. You can choose to walk away. You cannot live two stories at the same time. You have to choose.

After word got around that Jesus was performing great miracles, large crowds starting following Him and His disciples. Then Jesus started to teach and explain what living out the lost lines was going to involve and that there was a cost involved. At this, some started complaining that it was too hard. And then the Bible says, "From this time many of his disciples turned back and no longer followed him" (John 6:66).

The ones with divided hearts left. At first glance, it may seem like Jesus didn't do a good job of winning friends and influencing people that day. But the entire point of Jesus' teachings was to make a fair disclosure of the fact that we cannot follow Him long term with divided hearts. We are to love Him with all our hearts.

I attended film school for a little while, and the first lesson I learned was about the importance of the script. The key lesson the professors taught us was that you can make a bad movie out of a good script, *but you cannot make a good movie out of a bad script.*

And so it is with life. You cannot make a good life with a bad script. Or with two scripts.

William Barclay, the Scottish Bible teacher and commentator once wrote:

> **It is possible to be a follower of Jesus without being a disciple; to be a camp-follower without being a soldier of the king; to be a hanger-on in some great work without pulling one's weight. Once someone was talking to a great scholar about a younger man. He said, "So and so tells me that he was one of your students." The teacher answered devastatingly, "He may have attended my lectures, but he was not one of my students."**

Living our lost lines will mean being a true disciple of the Line-Giver, which in turn means we cannot live two scripts at the same time. How do we know if we are living a life straddling two scripts? How do we know whether we are living our lost lines or not?

You feel as though you have everything but possess nothing.

Your soul is bored, adrift, in despair.

Your soul is not only adrift but also devoid of joy, love, and peace.

Your life runs on one script on Sunday and another script on Monday.

You made some decisions years ago that were a degree or two off from the script of your life and you started to drift, and now, years later, you are way off course.

You have a low-grade anguish in your soul.

Your life is filled with things to do, schedules to keep, and errands to run, and you have the sense that your hope of doing something great is slowly fading away.

You lived your life according to a given script, and you are questioning whether or not it was the right script.

You are currently in a hard season in your life, and you struggle to see how you could be living your lost lines in it.

You have worked hard to build the life you have, only to realize it is not the life you want.

You live in a space where you are constantly dealing with the guilt of your yesterdays and the worries for your tomorrows. The net result is that you are unable to inhabit your todays.

And then there are times when we end up doing the wrong things for the right reasons. I see someone wanting so badly to live out their lost lines, to become the person God wants them to be. That's the right reason. But the way they go about it is to talk about themselves, their circumstances, and their views in ways that are meant to create an impression on others about who they would like to be. They work very hard to drop hints, innuendos, and lines, trying to create an impression of who they want people to think they are. But all this is hard work, and it has to be exhausting.

And Paul says you don't have to live that way anymore. God can and is willing to transform your story, to redeem your story, to give you the role of a lifetime.

Truth is, we live in this constant daily tension between the lure of the script of this world and the call of our soul to live our truest, most authentic selves by following the script of our Creator.

Following the Line-Giver means we walk closely with our Line-Giver. Our life is about discovering and learning and stretching and growing by following the Lord who calls us to a risky, sometimes demanding, often counter-cultural way of life.

> And living your lost lines means "normal" = 100-percent devotion.
> It means it's going to cost you something.
> It means denying ourselves and picking up our crosses daily.
> It means taking on the yoke of Jesus.
> It means talking to Him and following His lead every day.
> It means allowing Him access to every part of our lives.
> It means taking every thought captive and making it obedient to Christ.
> That's where the fullness of life is.

Anything else is settling for less than who we were
    meant to be.
There is no other way to lead a meaningful life. And if we
    believe that, then we must believe that every single
    day, not just Sunday, God is at work and He wants
    to make this day, whatever day it may be, glorious
    with our recognition of His presence, His power, His
    greatness, His grace, His lordship, His mercy and
    love and peace.
Normal = 100-percent devotion.

David put it this way, "Teach me your way, LORD, that I may rely on your faithfulness; give me an undivided heart, that I may fear your name" (Psalm 86:11).

David knew a thing or two about not living with a divided heart. The writer of 2 Kings adds this phrase about King Amaziah—he was not like David (2 Kings 14:3). David wasn't perfect, but he had a heart that was different from Amaziah's.

# Chapter 8

# HEART

The LORD looks at the heart.

—*1 Samuel 16:7*

Imagine yourself as a living house. God comes in to rebuild that house. At first, perhaps, you can understand what He is doing. He is getting the drains right and stopping the leaks in the roof and so on; you knew that those jobs needed doing and so you are not surprised. But presently He starts knocking the house about in a way that hurts abominably and does not seem to make sense. What on earth is He up to? The explanation is that He is building quite a different house from the one you thought of—throwing out a new wing here, putting on an extra floor there, running up towers, making courtyards. You thought you were going to be made into a decent little cottage: but He is building a palace. He intends to come and live in it Himself.

—*C. S. Lewis*, Mere Christianity

The Bible talks a lot about the heart—more than seven hundred times. It points out all kinds of hearts—the pure heart, the joyful heart, the loving heart, the hardened heart, the wicked heart, and so on. What is important to note is that when the Bible talks about the heart, it is not referring to the physical organ itself but the seat or center of our very being. It is like the CEO that operates all parts of our human life—emotions, thoughts, reflections, passions, purposes, endeavors, and so on.

If we are to receive and understand and live out our lost lines from our Line-Giver, we will need to prepare our hearts to receive them.

How do we prepare our hearts?
How does this help us receive our lost lines?
And what does that process look like?

These are great questions, and in attempt to answer them, I am going to take you through one part of the story of a man who cast a long shadow on the biblical narrative. His name was David.

His list of achievements are impressive—an accomplished musician whose songs are sung today even after three thousand years. He was a fearsome warrior and a great king. David received, understood, and lived out his lost lines. Reading the biblical narrative, we can glean hints as to how that happened.

The LORD said to Samuel, "How long will you mourn for Saul, since I have rejected him as king over Israel? . . . I am sending you to Jesse of Bethlehem. I have chosen one of his sons to be king." . . . Samuel did what the LORD said. . . . he consecrated Jesse and his sons and invited them to the sacrifice. When they arrived, Samuel saw Eliab and thought, "Surely the LORD's anointed stands here before the LORD." But the LORD said to Samuel, "Do not consider his appearance or his height, for

I have rejected him. The LORD does not look at the things people look at. People look at the outward appearance, but the LORD looks at the heart."

—*1 Samuel 16:1–13*

Three chapters earlier, Samuel tells Saul that "the LORD has sought out a man after his own heart" (1 Samuel 13:14).

God looks at the heart.
He looks at my heart. Your heart. David's heart.
And calls David, a man after God's own heart.
The Line-Giver is looking at hearts.
Open hearts.
Tuned-in hearts.
Humble hearts.
Searching hearts.
Committed hearts.

"The eyes of the LORD search the whole earth in order to strengthen those whose hearts are fully committed to him" (2 Chronicles 16:9 NLT).

Hearts ready to receive and obey and live out their lost lines.

The heart is such a precious thing—Scripture tells us to be careful what you give it to. Your whole life could be shaped by what you give your heart to. The very first Bible verse I taught my kids was, "Guard your heart above all else, for it determines the course of your life" (Proverbs 4:23 NLT).

Guard it intensely, passionately, fervently.
It's the only one you'll ever have.
Above everything else,
be extraordinarily protective of your heart.

Be extremely discriminating about who or what you give
    your heart to,
what you allow your heart to be drawn to,
what you expose your heart to,
how you allow your heart to be shaped and molded and
    fashioned and influenced,
for it will determine the course of your life.

Who or what you give your heart to will impact your
    choices.
It will guide your values.
It will shape your character.
It will influence your ability to discern and reason.
It will direct your thoughts and decisions and judgments.
It will impact and sway and pull you toward a certain way
    of living.
And so the Bible says, *this is a big deal*, above
    everything else,
above your wealth,
above your possessions,
above your titles and trophies and talents and awards,
*above everything else.*
Guard your heart,
be extremely careful what you give your heart to.
The entire course of your life depends on it.

Now, the world will offer a set of lines that are quite different. These lines will tell you something else entirely. Our world says to follow your heart. But then the Bible says, "The heart is deceitful above all things, and desperately wicked: who can know it?" (Jeremiah 17:9 KJV).

Or to use the amplified version, "The heart is deceitful above all things and it is extremely sick! Who can understand it fully and know its secret motives?" (Jeremiah 17:9 AMP).

To receive, understand, obey, and live out our lost lines, we will need to have our hearts set right. And unless our hearts are changed, we will, like Amaziah, remain either unchanged or divided in our hearts.

In his book *The Spirit of Disciplines*, Dallas Willard writes:

> **How many people are radically and permanently repelled from The Way by Christians who are unfeeling, stiff, unapproachable, boringly lifeless, obsessive, and dissatisfied? . . . "Spirituality" wrongly understood . . . is a major source of human misery and rebellion against God.**

Living our lost lines starts with a change of the heart. Once we understand who our Line-Giver is, we attune our hearts with His. Sometimes people think changing the externals will produce this kind of change and transformation. They get into all sorts of rules and guidelines and disciplines. It is possible to conform to all sorts of rules and guidelines and disciplines and gain human approval, but it amounts to nothing if the heart remains unchanged.

These people come near to me with their mouth and honor me with their lips, but their hearts are far from me. Their worship of me is based on merely human rules they have been taught.

—*Isaiah 29:13*

One day, an expert of the law came to Jesus with a question:

> "Teacher, which is the greatest commandment in the Law?" Jesus replied: "'Love the Lord your God with all your heart and with all your soul and with all your mind.' This is the first and greatest commandment. And the second is like it: 'Love your neighbor as yourself.' All the Law and the Prophets hang on these two commandments."
>
> —*Matthew 22:36–40*

Jesus said to love God and love people. Love God with all your heart. According to Jesus, that's the most amazing, remarkable, greatest thing you can do with your heart—give it fully to God. That's the first step to finding our lost lines. If you have not fully surrendered your heart to Christ, you will remain part of the unfeeling, stiff, unapproachable, obsessive, dissatisfied, and boringly lifeless group.

Jesus connected the outward displays of our lives with the heart. He explained it this way:

> Don't you see that whatever enters the mouth goes into the stomach and then out of the body? But the things that come out of a person's mouth come from the heart, and these defile them. For out of the heart come evil thoughts— murder, adultery, sexual immorality, theft, false testimony, slander.
>
> —*Matthew 15:17–19*

But, Jesus insists, true life and meaning and significance come our way when we surrender our imperfect human hearts fully to God, not just in designated places and times, but fully, every day—we become a people after God's own heart flowing with life-giving streams. In essence, living our lost lines.

How do go about cultivating a heart like that?

Let's go back to David for an answer to that question. It's an extraordinary statement—a man after God's own heart, a woman after God's own heart. What was it about David and his heart that captured the heart of God? Can you and I get a heart like David?

David had a heart that was wide open to God. Even a quick browsing of his life and writings makes this attribute stand out among others. He loved God and worshipped Him fully, passionately, and enthusiastically. He wrote repeatedly in Psalms about his heart for God. Let me walk you through a few of them.

My shield is God Most High, who saves the upright in heart.

—*Psalm 7:10*

I trust in your unfailing love; my heart rejoices in your salvation.

—*Psalm 13:5*

The precepts of the LORD are right, giving joy to the heart. . . . May the words of my mouth and this meditation of my heart be pleasing in your sight, LORD, my Rock and my Redeemer.

—*Psalm 19:8, 14*

My heart says of you, "Seek his face!"
Your face, Lord, I will seek.

—*Psalm 27:8*

My heart, O God, is steadfast; I will sing
and make music with all my soul.

—*Psalm 108:1*

His heart was on a relentless pursuit of God.

One time, he was worshipping and leaping and dancing with great intensity. His wife took him aside and scolded him—"How the king of Israel has distinguished himself today, going around half-naked in full view of the slave girls of his servants as any vulgar fellow would!" (2 Samuel 6:20). She thinks it's beneath the king's dignity to leap and dance and praise God that way.

And David's response was, are you kidding me? The actual words he used were, "I will celebrate before the Lord. I will become even more undignified than this" (vv. 21–22).

David had a fully devoted heart. That didn't mean he was flawless. His sins are almost as well known as his praise songs. But what it means is that he had a heart that was wide open to God.

Another time, he was getting ready to make an offering to God. There was a guy who wanted to offer him everything for free to do it—land, oxen, wood—but David said, "No, I insist on paying you for it. I will not sacrifice to the Lord my God . . . offerings that cost me nothing" (2 Samuel 24:24).

Can you imagine if every week we walked into our churches prepared to worship God with offerings that truly cost us something? What would that do to our hearts?

David's heart was filled with gratitude toward God (see Psalm 138, among others). He also loved God's Word.

Joyful are people of integrity, who follow the instructions of the Lord. Joyful are those who obey his laws and search for him with all their hearts.

—Psalm 119:1–2 NLT

How I delight in your commands! How I love them! I honor and love your commands. I meditate on your decrees.

—Psalm 119:47–48 NLT

Every step of the way, David not only sought God, but he gave God the credit as the ultimate Author of his lines. When facing Goliath, he famously uttered these words:

You come against me with sword and spear and javelin, but I come against you in the name of the Lord Almighty, the God of the armies of Israel, whom you have defied. . . . for the battle is the Lord's, and he will give all of you into our hands.

—1 Samuel 17:45–47

David was wide open to God, not just in designated places and times, but in his everyday life—when he was tending sheep, when he was in his palace, when he was hiding in a cave, when he was facing Goliath, when he was lying in a pasture. No place, circumstance, or time was a barrier to him remaining connected to his Line-Giver.

David had a heart that loved God with reckless abandon. The second thing about David's heart is that he loved deeply. He really cared about the community of God. Again, his writings reveal his heart.

How wonderful, how beautiful, when brothers and sisters get along! It's like costly anointing oil flowing down head and beard, flowing down Aaron's beard, flowing down the collar of his priestly robes. It's like the dew on Mount Hermon flowing down the slopes of Zion. Yes, that's where GOD commands the blessing, ordains eternal life.

*—Psalm 133 The Message*

The clearest sign of David's love for the community of God was his love for his friend Jonathan. Even after Jonathan's death, he welcomed Jonathan's crippled son and gave him a seat at the king's table. His heart swelled with love for the house of God, "One thing I ask from the LORD, this only do I seek: that I may dwell in the house of the LORD all the days of my life, to gaze on the beauty of the LORD and to seek him in his temple" (Psalm 27:4).

I want a heart like that. So do you. But we cannot have that heart all by ourselves. We will need to guard it, submit it, and surrender it to the Line-Giver.

So we ask the Line-Giver
to search our hearts (Psalm 139:23),
to cleanse our hearts (Psalm 51:2), and
to give us a new heart (Ezekiel 36:26),
for his lines to be written in our hearts (Jeremiah 31:33).

When you have the Line-Giver dwell in your hearts,
then you will be rooted and grounded in love,
and start to grasp how wide and long and high and deep
    is the love of Christ,
and be filled to the measure of all the fullness of God
    (Ephesians 3:17–19).

A heart like David's is so tuned into God that uncommon boldness, radical faithfulness, and unshakeable love become the hallmarks of such a heart. A heart like that will worship a God that is bigger than all the lions and bears and Goliaths the world can bring. It will beat with a rhythm of grace and love toward people. It will pulsate with passionate worship and bold prayers. It will be filled with a breathtaking vision walking in tandem with a God whose will will be done and whose kingdom will come on earth as it is in heaven.

# Chapter 9

# SIMULCAST

Everything that goes into a life of pleasing God has been miraculously given to us by getting to know, personally and intimately, the One who invited us to God. The best invitation we ever received!

—*2 Peter 1:3 The Message*

Whatever man may stand, whatever he may do, to whatever he may apply his hand—in agriculture, in commerce, and in industry, or his mind, in the world of art, and science—he is, in whatsoever it may be, constantly standing before the face of God. He is employed in the service of his God. He has strictly to obey his God. And above all, he has to aim at the glory of his God.

—*Abraham Kuyper, as quoted in* Honey from the Lion: Christian Theology and the Ethics of Nationalism, *by Doug Gay*

get some variation of these questions all the time:

I understand our Line-Giver created us and gave us our lost lines, and I see many examples in the Bible of God speaking to people. And then there

are prophets and signs and wonders and divine
revelation. But what about us and what about me
and what about now? Is God still as active, and
does He still speak like He did with people in those
stories in the Bible?

If the answer to the first question is yes, explain how and
why so many people ignore the chance to receive
and live their lost lines?

What do I need to know and do to live a life that
receives and lives the lost lines, and how do I avoid
becoming someone who either doesn't receive or
receives but does not live out the lost lines for one
reason or another?

Perhaps a parable might help.

Jesus was a master storyteller, and He often spoke in parables.
We don't use the word *parable* much in our day, but it is actually
made up of two words that mean to "to cast" and "close beside,
with." So Jesus would cast out a masterfully crafted story (from the
stuff of daily life) and then cast a great spiritual truth alongside it. It
is like someone sharing a great story with an even greater point.

And so it is that one day Jesus shared a story. A large crowd
had gathered, and Jesus got on a boat and sat down while the
crowd stood on the shore. Perhaps there was a farmer working on a
field nearby because Jesus chose a common sight of those days and
wove a story about a sower and seeds and soil. And we'll come back
to the story in a moment, but look at the way Jesus ends the story,
"Whoever has ears, let them hear" (Matthew 13:9).

Jesus used the word *hear* more than a dozen times in this
chapter, and it is also sprinkled throughout all Scripture. All the way
back in Deuteronomy 6, Moses gives the Israelites some powerful

set of instructions for living their lost lines. He started off by saying the people were to remember and learn and teach what he was about to say, and then he says this (the entire chapter 6 is worth a slow and meditative read):

> Hear, O Israel: The LORD our God, the LORD is one. Love the LORD your God with all your heart and with all your soul and with all your strength.
>
> —*Deuteronomy 6:4–5*

It became part of the prayer called *Shema*. It is a powerful affirmation of who God is, and for thousands of years, millions of Jews have prayed this prayer daily.

Now that word *shema* is actually a very common word and occurs more than a thousand times in the Bible. It is the word that starts the passage above and is translated as "hear" in verse 4. But the word *shema* is also translated as another word elsewhere. At the end of the Book of Joshua, for instance, Joshua charged the people to follow God wholeheartedly. The people responded, "We will serve the LORD our God and obey him" (Joshua 24:24).

That word *obey* is the same word translated "hear" in Deuteronomy 6. And the reason for this is that in the context of the Bible, hearing and obeying are intricately connected. So when the prophet Jeremiah says, "Hear this now, O foolish people, without understanding, who have eyes and see not, and who have ears and hear not" (Jeremiah 5:21 NKJV), he doesn't mean the people couldn't actually see and hear. They did see and they could hear, but they chose not to obey and follow. Later on in the New Testament, James would exhort us to not just be hearers of the word but be doers (James 1:22).

So when Jesus said whoever has ears to hear, let him hear, what it meant was that Jesus was not only calling the people to pay attention to what He was saying but to stop, seek to understand, *and* obey and follow. For that is where finding, understanding, *and* living our lost lines happens.

This is an important context through which we will now look at the densely packed story Jesus masterfully crafted:

> A farmer went out to sow his seed. As he was scattering the seed, some fell along the path, and the birds came and ate it up. Some fell on rocky places, where it did not have much soil. It sprang up quickly, because the soil was shallow. But when the sun came up, the plants were scorched, and they withered because they had no root. Other seed fell among thorns, which grew up and choked the plants. Still other seed fell on good soil, where it produced a crop—a hundred, sixty or thirty times what was sown. Whoever has ears, let them hear.
>
> *—Matthew 13:3–9*

Let's start with the farmer. There's something strange and unique and fascinating about him. He scatters seeds, but he follows what at first glance appears to be a rather silly method. He is not being very careful about where exactly He plants the seeds. This is a farmer who is so extravagantly generous, He scatters seeds everywhere.

The farmer, or the sower, in this story is our Line-Giver. The seed is the Word of God or the gospel or our lost lines. The different types of soil represent the conditions of our hearts and our receptiveness to the Line-Giver's gift.

The entire story is about the bigheartedness and extravagance of the Line-Giver. In fact, this method of seeding is often referred to as broadcast seeding (*casting* seeds over a *broad* area). The Line-Giver is so generous that He broadcasts, in effect simulcasting, our lost lines all over the place. He is not being stingy with it. He does not hold back and give the lines only to those who are willing to listen. It is there, available for anyone. But as the story unfolds, we find anyone can get to the seeds, the lost lines, but not everyone does. They have eyes, but they don't see. They have ears, but they don't hear.

So Jesus made it exceedingly clear. He said some people hear about the good news, the seeds of the gospel, their lost lines, but their hearts are like a well-worn path. The soil is tightly packed and there is resistance to growth. Maybe they have been abused or have experienced pain or are hurting and are discouraged and disappointed and distrustful. And they have allowed these things to harden their hearts, creating a defensive shield of cynicism. They may hear their lost lines, but Jesus said the evil one comes and takes it away (v. 19). The lines do not have a chance because the hearts are not soft enough for the lines to take root. And a chance to live a fruitful life is lost.

The second type of soil is referred to as shallow and rocky. It represents hearts that receive their lost lines with great joy and at least for a season it looks as though they are living their lost lines. But their hearts are shallow and superficial. The soil is not deep. So the seeds never form deep roots. So much of our current world is about superficiality.

Writing in 1985, educator Neil Postman made this commentary about Americans in his book *Amusing Ourselves to Death*:

**Americans no longer talk to each other, they entertain each other. They do not exchange ideas, they exchange images. They do not argue with propositions; they argue with good looks, celebrities, and commercials.**

Our shallow commitments, our isolation from meaningful community, and the triviality of most of our social media posts all point to superficial hearts. There aren't any deep connections, strong commitments, or profound convictions. These things do not happen in shallow soil. And when things get hard, Jesus said, they wilt. They had a moment when they experienced what it was like to live their lost lines. But not any more. Now life flits from one thing to another—another job, another church, another marriage, another friend. The soil needs to be soft, and the soil needs to be deep for the roots to develop.

The third type of heart or soil has the right softness and depth, but the problem is of another kind. Jesus said thorns or weeds grew up and choked the plants. It represents people who received their lost lines. They understood them and put them into practice. They started listening and obeying and seeing the fruit the Line-Giver wants to give. But they allowed other voices and lines to seep into their lives. They didn't set the dial on the channel of the Line-Giver. They hit the scan button and kept switching from channel to channel. Their hearts were right, but they were scattered in their devotion. Soon, the channel of the Line-Giver is tuned out, and the other voices, the other noises and the other forms of chatter, overtake their lost lines and choke them out.

Distractions, chatter, and noise are everywhere. And they crop up like weeds and thorns and choke out the life-giving lines the Line-Giver wants us to live.

Maybe the soil of your heart is like a well-worn path. You hear Him offering you your lost lines, but you resist. You've let people walk all over you, and now you have hardened your heart. You don't want to be hurt again. Perhaps you had a vision for your life, but things turned out to be very different, and you are bitterly disappointed. Maybe someone let you down. You feel betrayed and rejected and unwanted. And so you have put on a strong shield over your heart. No one can hurt you anymore.

You cannot live your lost lines if you refuse to allow them to penetrate your heart. A seed can't grow in hard soil. But all one single seed needs is a tiny crack. Would you be open to softening the soil of your heart? Would you allow a seed to fall through a crack? This seed, the Word of God, containing your lost lines, is packed with life and power. It is powerful and active and living beyond anything you can imagine. All it takes is one crack, one prayer, one step. The Line-Giver's promise is this: "I will give you a new heart, and I will put a new spirit in you. I will take out your stony, stubborn heart and give you a tender, responsive heart" (Ezekiel 36:26 NLT).

Maybe the soil of your heart is like the shallow soil of a rocky landscape. And you can remember the time when you first received the good news and understood your lost lines. But soon life turned into one crazy busy way of living. You have no solid friendships or community you belong to. You have no one you can go to and talk about the deep things of life. Maybe you are in the midst of a crisis that has brought this to light. Jesus said when trouble hits, the lines sown in shallow soil wilt.

The good news is that it is possible to turn shallow soil into deep soil. Start with the Line-Giver. Get to know Him in prayer and live in the awareness of His presence and His desire to speak into every facet of your life. Cling to His promise to never leave you or forsake you (Hebrews 13:5). Truth is, *you* ignored *Him*. Allow the seed of the Word to sink deeply. Intentionally make room for your local church and neighbors and others where you can start to form deeper relational connections. The thing about going deeper is that it takes time.

Maybe the soil of your heart is the one filled with thorns and weeds. You have the softness and the depth. You received and understood your lost lines, but you have allowed too many voices to stream into your life. Now the Line-Giver is just one voice among many. It starts in such a subtle way. Jesus calls it the worries of this life (Mark 4:19). Maybe it's stuff. You have too many things, and keeping up with everything takes so much of your time and attention. Maybe you used to be connected to a church community, but one day you decided to stay home from church because you had a hard week or your kids had a game on Sunday morning. That one weekend turned to months, and now you only sporadically attend church. You can sense the lost lines being choked out of you and your family.

Maybe it's debt and bad financial habits. Perhaps it's time to enroll in a financial management class and meet with someone who can help you get your financial house in order. Maybe it's sacrificing relationships and family for career and success and bigger salaries that keeps you and your heart and mind engaged primarily at maintaining the current level of your status.

Thorns, weeds—if you allow it, they will grow without hindrance. One of the most tragic things in life is to succeed spectacularly in living out your wrong lines. The good news is you can do some gardening work right now. Decide right now to keep the Line-Giver and your lost lines central to your life. Reclaim the script of your life.

Jesus now moves to the climax of the story, which He has been building up masterfully. He ends His story by talking about the fourth type of soil, or hearts—the good and fertile soil. This soil is the heart wide open and attentive to the one channel that truly matters. It receives and understands and cultivates and lives out the lost lines. It evaluates all decisions and commitments and choices in light of the life we were meant to live.

When such a heart receives the seed, the Word, its lost lines, it grows deep roots because the soil is deep and soft and open to receiving. Such a heart loves God, loves people, loves God's Word and community and mission. The result is that such a life will produce a tremendous amount of fruit—thirty, sixty, a hundredfold.

The harvest of good works in and through such a life will be of unimaginable significance. Our Line-Giver also said:

> I am the vine; you are the branches. If you remain in me and I in you, you will bear much fruit; apart from me you can do nothing.
> —*John 15:5*

Once we discover, understand, and live our lost lines, we are not only soil, but we get to join the Farmer in sowing the seeds of the gospel in others. We get to introduce others to their lost lines! And some will not respond well. They may have a hardened heart or shallow heart or a thorn-infested heart. But you never know. Some seeds will fall on good soil, and then you will simply be stunned when the harvest comes.

Our Line-Giver is simulcasting the message about our lost lines. He says things like:

> The thief comes only to steal and kill and destroy; I have come that they may have life, and have it to the full.
> —*John 10:10*

The Line-Giver has not changed. Our lost lines have not changed. So then fruitfulness and an abundant life depends very much on the condition of the soil—meaning whether we listen and understand and live out our lost lines. The only variable in the story is the soil— our response to our lost lines.

What is amazing about our Line-Giver is that He is so extravagantly generous. He will not withhold the lost lines from someone who has been hard-hearted and rejected Him. He keeps giving, keeps scattering the seed, keeps broadcasting the lost lines in a global nonstop simulcast. Perhaps a seed will fall through the crack and bring life and healing. He does not withhold the lost lines from those who once loved Him and had received their lost lines with such joy but are not living in them now. He keeps scattering the seed, keeps broadcasting the lost lines, and keeps giving. Perhaps they will turn around and listen and obey and find the joy and meaning they are missing out on. He does not withhold the lost lines from someone who has allowed their lost lines to be drowned in a chorus of voices, pursued the lines of this world, and been weighed down by the worries of this world. He keeps scattering the seed, keeps broadcasting the lost lines, and keeps giving. Perhaps a seed will break through the chatter and buzz.

Whoever has ears, let them hear.

# Chapter 10

# AMAZED

Many, Lord my God, are the wonders you have done, the things you planned for us. None can compare with you; were I to speak and tell of your deeds, they would be too many to declare

—*Psalm 40:5*

The people who hanged Christ never, to do them justice, accused Him of being a bore—on the contrary, they thought Him too dynamic to be safe. It has been left for later generations to muffle up that shattering personality and surround Him with an atmosphere of tedium.

—*Dorothy L. Sayers,* Letters to a Diminished Church

If we stop long enough to look around, one of the things we will notice a lot in our culture is people engaging in mindless entertainment, games, addictions, reaching out at every distraction, interruption, push notification, email alert, and diversion. I think part of the reason is that we have so much affluence, so many options, so many of our basic needs are met that, if truth be told, many of us are just plain bored with life.

Or as Leo Tolstoy defines it in *Anna Karenina*, this boredom is the "desire for desires." And when we don't find the right lines, our lost lines to fulfill this desire of our souls, we get bored. We are not talking about being silent or quiet retreating and seeking times of contemplation. We are talking about being in that place and space in our lives where there is no excitement, there are no hills to take, there is no significance, no meaning, no thrill, no enthusiasm, no exhilaration of giving our lives for the pursuit of worthy goals.

According to *Reuters*, a large survey of 81,000 students from twenty-six states, found that two-thirds of high school students say they are bored *every single day*. Researchers at University College London studying more than seven thousand civil servants over twenty-five years found that those who were bored were nearly 40 percent more likely to have died by the end of the study than those who did not. It seems you can, quite literally, be bored to death.

The lines our world gives us to live will eventually lead to emptiness and boredom. When there is no higher goal, no higher calling, no meaningful purpose, and we are bored, we start looking for ways to feel some excitement, something to stimulate our senses, something to ignite our soul so we can feel alive, even for a few moments.

In the movie *Jurassic World*, there is a scene where a team of potential sponsors for the Jurassic World theme park is being shown around when the character Claire asks them what they really want.

"We want to be thrilled," says one of them.

"Don't we all?" she responds.

We look to regain a sense of awe and wonder and amazement that the gnawing low frequency signal of our soul says we were created to live and experience. And yet, so many people are living lines that are devoid of life, awe, and wonder. Some have a sense that the lines they were handed and are living feel and look downright dull, desperate, and insipid. It is the script of a reductionist life that is gloomy and mundane and uninspired playing out in monochrome. The Christian life without a sense of awe and wonder and surprise and amazement and reverence is a life full of inert faith, calcified religion, and ineffective ideology.

And Paul insists that in Jesus there is this transformation available through the renewing of our minds in Christ. The word *transformed* in Romans 12:2 is translated from a word from which we get the word *metamorphosis*. When we think of that word, the image that comes to our mind is that of a butterfly. It used to be an ugly caterpillar crawling in the dirt, stuck in the mud, unable to see beyond what's immediately in front of it. But it went through this remarkable transformation to become a beautiful butterfly flying above the dirt, searching for the flowers, and able to see greater distances.

We were designed and crafted to rise above the dirt and mud. Abraham Joshua Heschel writes in his book *God in Search of Man*:

> **Our goal should be to live life in radical amazement . . .**
> **get up in the morning and look at the world in a way**
> **that takes nothing for granted. Everything is**
> **phenomenal; everything is incredible; never treat**
> **life casually. *To be spiritual is to be amazed.***
> **(Emphasis added.)**

Which brings to mind a scene out of Acts 2 about the early church.

They devoted themselves to the apostles' teaching and to fellowship, to the breaking of bread and to prayer. *Everyone was filled with awe* at the many wonders and signs performed by the apostles. All the believers were together and had everything in common. They sold property and possessions to give to anyone who had need.

Every day they continued to meet together in the temple courts. They broke bread in their homes and ate together with glad and sincere hearts, praising God and enjoying the favor of all the people. And the Lord added to their number daily those who were being saved.

*—Acts 2:42–47 (Emphasis added.)*

This is a remarkable set of words, and they have inspired millions of people over hundreds of years. The community Jesus started was so amazing, so transcendent, so much bigger than anything else, that these people were, the text tells us, *filled with awe.*

This awe wasn't a weekly fix they got when they went to church and sang a few songs and heard a message. It was a lifestyle of being in awe. A way of life. They experienced this sense of awe, this life of awe, this mindset of awe, not just one day but the next and the next and the next.

Wonderful, amazing, miraculous, remarkable things were happening. As I walk with Jesus, the Line-Giver, as my Lord and Savior, am I living a life characterized by a sense of awe? Is there a sense of anticipation that marks the beginning of each day? Have I retained that childlike sense of amazement?

I think a lot of us struggle with this.
There was a time when we were so full of awe and
    wonder, maybe it was our childhood.
And now, we are living day to day and,
it is hard to imagine a sense of wonder.
It is hard to imagine a sense of awe.
Life feels quite drab and insipid.
And we wonder if we will ever gain that sense of awe back.

Søren Kierkegaard writes in his essay "The Present Age," "The present age is essentially a sensible age, devoid of passion." And when we live a life devoid of passion and awe and wonder, we start praying informational prayers of little faith. We start worshipping without exuberant joy, and we start living a life without much hope but filled with fear and worry and anxiety.

Many of us as children inhabited a world rich in awe and wonder and then we grew old and lost that sense of being radically amazed, to not take things for granted, to not treat life so casually, to live our lost lines with a sense of awe and wonder.

I believe the lines our world hands us will lead us to a profound loss of a sense of awe and wonder. Which is why staying close to the Line-Giver on a daily basis is critical.

I see this sometimes. Christianity can start off with excitement and sense of awe and mystery, and then the needle on our awe-meter starts slipping. And God becomes familiar and ordinary and normal and frankly not all that exceptional. He becomes predictable, convenient, and functional. To be called upon as needed.

We get bored. And we start to die a little.

Swedish diplomat and author Dag Hammarskjöld once wrote:

**God does not die on the day when we cease to believe in a personal deity. But we die on the day when our lives cease to be illumined by the steady radiance, renewed daily, of a wonder, the source of which is beyond all reason.**

One of my deepest passions that keep me in ministry is actually one of the things I deeply detest. I detest it when people say they are not a follower of Christ or that they don't go to church because it's boring. As a pastor and a preacher, that just gets under my skin. *Nobody ever said that about Jesus.*

The woman at the well found a gentle Jesus.
Nicodemus found a patient Jesus.
The Pharisees found an indignant Jesus.
The children found a loving Jesus.
The moneychangers found an angry Jesus.
Zacchaeus found an accepting and gracious Jesus.
Nobody ever found a boring Jesus. You know why?
*Because boring Jesus doesn't exist.*

People were attracted by Jesus,
loved by Jesus,
accepted by Jesus,
stunned by Jesus,
transformed by Jesus,
captivated by Jesus,
healed by Jesus,
irritated by Jesus,
angered by Jesus.
Nobody was ever bored by Jesus.

If we are truly walking closely with Jesus, if the church is truly preaching the Jesus of the Gospels, and if we truly find and live our lost lines, then no one can ever say the movement Jesus started is boring, dull, lifeless, or insipid.

Contrast this with how many times the Gospels record a moment when people were amazed with Jesus. If you read the Gospel accounts of the life of Jesus, wherever He went, He left people amazed. It didn't matter if they were young or old, male or female, Jew or Gentile, rich or poor, or believed in Him or not. They were all amazed.

Let's walk through a few scenes (emphasis added):

> When Jesus had finished saying these things, the crowds were *amazed* at his teaching.
>
> —*Matthew 7:28*

> The men were *amazed* and asked, "What kind of man is this? Even the winds and the waves obey him!"
>
> —*Matthew 8:27*

> The people were *amazed* at his teaching, because he taught them as one who had authority, not as the teachers of the law.
>
> —*Mark 1:22*

> The crowd was *amazed* and said, "Nothing like this has ever been seen in Israel."
>
> —*Matthew 9:33*

> All spoke well of him and were *amazed* at the gracious words that came from his lips.
>
> —*Luke 4:22*

> This *amazed* everyone and they praised God, saying, "We have never seen anything like this!"
>
> —*Mark 2:12*

The people were *amazed* when they saw the mute speaking, the crippled made well, the lame walking and the blind seeing. And they praised the God of Israel.

—*Matthew 15:31*

When the disciples saw this, they were *amazed*.

—*Matthew 21:20*

The disciples were *amazed* at his words.

—*Mark 10:24*

The whole crowd was *amazed*.

—*Mark 11:18*

And they were *amazed* at him.

—*Mark 12:17*

Pilate was *amazed*.

—*Mark 15:5*

Everyone was *amazed* and gave praise to God. They were filled with *awe*.

—*Luke 5:26*

It just goes on and on. Jesus left a trail of amazement wherever He went. People who were hanging out with Jesus, learning their lost lines from Him, understanding His way of life and living it, were in this frequent state of amazement.

We live in this hypertext, hyperspeed, hyperconnected world where it is easy to lose our compass. And the tragedy is that we become a people devoid of any passion and awe and wonder.

As a prayer in a Jewish prayer book says:

**Days pass and the years vanish and we walk sightless among miracles. Lord, fill our eyes with seeing and our minds with knowing. . . . Help us to see, wherever we gaze, that the bush burns, unconsumed.**

The Psalmist writes:

O LORD, our Lord, your majestic name fills the earth! Your glory is higher than the heavens. . . . When I look at the night sky and see the work of your fingers—the moon and the stars you set in place—what are mere mortals that you should think about them, human beings that you should care for them?

—*Psalm 8:1, 3–4 NLT*

We live in a cynical age and in a cynical world that is filled with cynical talking heads. We have eyes, but we cannot see. The prophets talked about our blindness and deafness (see Isaiah 6:9–10; Jeremiah 5:21; and Ezekiel 12:2) and Jesus repeats their teaching in Matthew 13:13–15. Paul reiterates it in Acts 28:27. It is possible to have eyes and look, but not see. To walk past the bush that burns unconsumed.

Helen Keller wrote a beautiful article about this same idea in *The Atlantic*. One day, a friend visited her. As the woman had just returned from a walk in the woods, Keller asked her what she observed. Her friend replied, "Nothing in particular." Keller is incredulous. How is it possible to have sight and not see? She then imagines what it would be like to have sight for three days. She makes an extensive itinerary of the three days. In a poignant pouring of her heart, she describes in detail all the things she would see if she had sight. She would gaze at the face of her loved ones, watch a baby, see her dogs, the colors of her rug, read books, walk in the woods and take in the splendor of nature, gaze at the dawn, watch theater and visit museums, and watch people in New York. She exhorts the reader to not just look, but see.

Living a life of amazement would mean rising above the smog-filled world of the caterpillar, finding our lost lines, living them, and doing a surgical removal of cynicism from our hearts.

Perhaps one way to find that sense of amazement is to do what Helen Keller did and make our list of things that amaze us. I want to encourage you to make your own amazed list—things that fill you with a sense of amazement and wonder. Here are some things that fill me with amazement:

> The energy of a beautiful song, the color of fall leaves,
>     the mysterious capacity of Sharpies and Post-it
>     Notes to spark creativity.
> Indian food, libraries, and mountains.
> The Smithsonian and the Lincoln Memorial.
> Books and movies about people succeeding in the face
>     of impossible odds.
> Traveling to another country and experiencing a different
>     culture on God's good earth.
> These words by Dallas Willard in his devotional *Hearing
>     God Through the Year*, "If our gospel does not
>     free the individual up for a unique life of spiritual

adventure in living with God daily, we simply have not entered fully into the good news that Jesus brought." And also this caution from his book *The Spirit of Disciplines*, "The greatest danger to the Christian church today is that of pitching its message too low."

And of course the list doesn't end there. I am amazed that a little over twenty years ago I asked the woman I was deeply in love with to marry me, and she actually said yes! I am amazed at (and delighted by) Erika's fiercely protective love of me and our children and how she daily and selflessly gives of herself to take care of us as a family. I'm amazed by her creative energy and joyous spirit.

I am filled with amazement when I think about my four daughters.

By Elizabeth. At how quickly my little girl has turned into a beautiful young woman. Her poise, her maturity of thinking, her laughter, her creativity, her sense of judgment, her inclusiveness, her energizing joyful spirit.

By Ashlynne. At her ability to reason, her mind, her imagination, her passion for books and classics and Jane Austen and Sherlock Holmes, her piano and songwriting skills, her intellectual and emotional maturity beyond her years.

By Ayanna. At her deep intensity, being either 100 percent fully committed or not at all. Her spirit of generosity, authenticity, and dedication. Her relentless focus and follow-through. Her intensity of spirit makes me wonder about the amazing things she will do with her life if she continues to stay rooted and grounded in Jesus.

By little Amber. At her charming and endearing personality, her sense of sharing, her curious mind, her smile, her nurturing attitude, her empathy for others.

I am filled with amazement at the community Jesus founded. By the epic diversity of people gathered at the church—Jews, Gentiles, male, female, Republicans, Democrats, Tea Partyists, pagans, law enforcement officers, former inmates, AA members, CEOs, people with doctorates and people with high school diplomas, boomers and millennials, bikers with leather jackets and seniors in their Sunday best—they all gather in unity under the banner of the Cross.

I stand in deep amazement of people who face such long odds, such unbearable pain like fear, anxiety, terminal illness, bankruptcies, broken marriages, unemployment, rejection, betrayal—I am amazed by the people who tackle these things and face another day with such enduring courage. These are the people who dance daily on the edge of a volcano, and it is poignant and profound and beautiful.

I am filled with awestruck wonder at the narrative of the poor Carpenter from Nazareth, the Son of the Living God becoming the final sacrifice, taking on the Cross for me (for you), but then breaking through the tomb, rising from the dead, and defeating death, sin, and guilt. How He sustains all things, reconciles all things, redeems all things.

And that this awesome, powerful, amazing God actually loves me!
A lot!
No matter what!
*Seriously amazing!*

Make your own awe list. I say this because if you think your life is boring and dull, maybe you need to lift your head up and look up from the ground. Pause long enough to notice the mystery and awe and wonder that God brings your way but which you do not notice. And you pass by the bush that burns unconsumed.

**Do something.**
**Find a place to serve at your church, in your community,**
   **in your home.**

Find a place to serve anywhere.

Go to serve.gov and support a military family.

Attempt something great.

Speak life into someone.

Make some goals.

Pray intensely.

Take control of your health.

Take control of your finances.

Dive into a ministry.

Go on a mission trip. Go on any trip.

Seek God's mind.

Go out on a limb.

Spread some joy.

Share some love.

Serve at a soup kitchen.

Sponsor a kid. Teach children about Jesus. Plant grand
visions in the life of a child.

Get involved.

Get engaged.

Get interested.

To paraphrase G. K. Chesterton, there is no such thing as an uninteresting life, only uninterested people. As we take this journey of discovery to find our lost lines, one of the things we will notice is it will fill our lives with the amazement with which we were created to live. We will be called to lay aside the mindset and attitudes and the script of our old lives and adopt a new mind, a new attitude, and a whole new outlook on life.

There is another place Paul used the same word for *transformation* as he did in Romans 12:2—it is found in 2 Corinthians 3:17–18:

> Now the Lord is the Spirit, and where the
> Spirit of the Lord is, there is freedom. And we all,

who with unveiled faces contemplate the Lord's glory, are being transformed into his image with ever-increasing glory, which comes from the Lord, who is the Spirit.

As we understand and live out our lost lines and walk in amazement with our Lord, we will increasingly conform into His image! That should fill us with amazement!

And that is where the discovery of our lost lines begins.

# Chapter 11

# DISCOVERY

He has saved us and called us to a holy life—not because of anything we have done but because of his own purpose and grace. This grace was given us in Christ Jesus before the beginning of time.

—*2 Timothy 1:9*

The important thing is this: to be able, at any moment, to sacrifice what we are for what we could become.

—*Charles Du Bos*

The road to discovery starts with recognizing that we have been victims of a massive fraud. We've been targets of an identity theft at a colossal scale. The lines we have been handed—*we can be like God*—are a lie.

Discovering our lost lines requires us to come to the Author of our script and allow Him to clean us from the inside out. We need to confess our dirt to Him and allow Him to clean the buckets of our soul.

Consider someone who grew up learning some old lines and imagined his or her life to be a certain way. And that person now wants to live the lost lines. It begins by recognizing you grew up learning some things you now need to *unlearn* and then *relearn* your new lines.

Jesus was constantly redirecting the lines. He would say things like, "You've heard . . ." or, "You are . . ."—that's the life you are living. And then He would say, "But I tell you . . ."—this is how life is meant to be. These are the lost lines. He would remind people about them. This is who you are. This is who you were meant to be, this is your story.

He came in contact with people who were entrenched in a different story, spouting lines they were not created to speak or live. And Jesus would call them out. He called out a Pharisee named Nicodemus (John 3) and a tax collector named Matthew (Matthew 9:9–13). There was Simon (John 1:35–42), who Jesus gave a new name and a new mission.

There were so many people from so many different walks of life and in every instance, Jesus would point them to the life they were meant to live. In essence, giving them their lost lines.

If you read the Bible, you will find that from Genesis to Revelation, God reminds us of our lost lines again and again and again. And when individuals listen and love and follow God with all their hearts, entire families, communities, and even nations are transformed.

God went to Abram and told him the script he was living did not contain the lines he was meant to live. He offers him his lost lines and a new nation is born.

God went to Moses and asked him to trade his lines of being a shepherd to some sheep and become the shepherd of an entire nation and lead them out of slavery.

God went to Gideon, who had come to believe the lines the world had handed him—that he was weak and fearful and discouraged. God gave him his lost lines of a mighty warrior. There's Joshua, Caleb, Saul, David, Nehemiah, Esther, Jonah, John Mark, Peter, Paul—the list goes on and on.

Then there's Augustine, Brother Lawrence, Johannes Gutenberg, Martin Luther, Blaise Pascal, William Carey, Francis of Assisi, David Livingstone, John Wesley, Charles Spurgeon, Dwight L. Moody, C. S. Lewis, Dorothy L. Sayers, Billy Graham, Mother Teresa, and Martin Luther King Jr. We could fill this whole book full of names. They were all captivated by the Line-Giver and His promise of giving us our lost lines.

We see this transformation again and again. Throughout Scripture and throughout history, people are living the lines they were handed or that they thought belonged to them or the ones the world thrusts upon them. And then the Living God, the Creator and Sustainer of every human life, comes along and offers them their lost lines. And when people listen and follow and obey, remarkable things happen. This profound, mysterious, and powerful partnership between God and passionate, determined, and obedient souls living their lost lines creates a rupture in the kingdom of this world. And a new way, a new life, a new dynamic breaks in.

This is not a three-step formula. Every story is different. We begin in prayer and God's Word. We have the grand story of the Bible. That is the big story, the grand story, the overarching narrative. We are united in our big story. But our individual stories, our individual lines, are unique to who God created us to be. He has gifted us differently, we are in different walks of life, and we are experiencing different things. God's goal through all of that is we live out our lost lines.

Living the kind of life the Line-Giver has designed for us cannot be abridged, hurried, or compressed. And it cannot be lived in isolation but must always be lived in community (more on that in chapter 15). But once we understand the difference between our given lines and our lost lines, and who our Line-Giver is, here are three things we can do at the start of our journey to discovering our lost lines.

First, we must look at a particular trait of the Line-Giver. It's found in Jeremiah 33:3. The Line-Giver says, "Call to me and I will answer you and tell you great and unsearchable things you do not know."

I have read, recited, and prayed this verse many times. The Bible is filled with words like *hunger*, *desire*, *pining*, *restlessness*, *seeking*, *thirst*, and *yearning*. These are profound words. They stir up the deep places of our souls. We yearn for the great and unsearchable things, our lost lines being one of them. Some translations interpret the word *unsearchable* as *mysterious*, *incomprehensible*, and *hidden*—our lost lines are impossible to live without God.

And God says: *Call to Me.*

My part of the deal is to call on Him. His part of the deal is to show me my lost lines. Here is the astounding paradox—we are searching for the One who is searching for us! There is this attribute of God, our Line-Giver, who so wants to get into a deep relational community with us and give us our lost lines. He repeats this refrain throughout Scripture.

Call on me in the day of trouble; I will deliver you, and you will honor me.

—*Psalm 50:15*

Before they call I will answer; while they are still speaking I will hear.

—*Isaiah 65:24*

Call on me and come and pray to me, and I will listen to you.

—*Jeremiah 29:12*

For there is no difference between Jew and Gentile—the same Lord is Lord of all and richly blesses all who call on him.

—*Romans 10:12*

That's the ache in God's heart. He looks at us and the way we live our lives, and He sees it all. He sees we are thirsty, dry, weary, and withered. He sees the condition of our soul. He is familiar with all our ways. He sees the pain. He sees the hardships. He sees the troubles. He sees us adorn fake masks and project a persona so far removed from the real us. He sees how we get enticed and deceived by the lines our world offers us. He sees all the grumbling and complaining. He sees all the junk coming off us living our old lines. He sees how we keep ourselves enslaved by choosing our own way, by living the script of the world.

He sees it all.

And He says, "Call to Me. I am here. I'll always be here." Jesus said, "Come to Me."

That's the very first step—come to Jesus. And do what He tells you to do. Because your lost lines are with Jesus. Scriptures tell us to "[fix] our eyes on Jesus the author and perfecter of our faith" (Hebrews 12:2 NASB).

Your lost lines are with Jesus because He wrote the screenplay. The word *author* can also be translated *originator*, *founder*, or *leader*. He not only wrote our lost lines, He can lead, guide, and direct us in living them. Interestingly, the word *perfecter* can also be translated *completer* or *finisher*. Jesus is not only the author of your lost lines, He can help you finish your story well! Which is why Paul wrote to the church in Philippi, "I am sure of this, that he who began a good work in you will bring it to completion at the day of Jesus Christ" (Philippians 1:6 ESV).

If we are to live the lost lines of our lives, we have to start here, with Jesus. If we stay rooted and grounded in Him and stay deep in prayer and His Word, living this life as part of His community, then we will live the lives we were meant to live. He longs to give you and me our lost lines.

The choice is still up to us. You can come to Jesus and find your lost lines, but the choice is still yours. You can still choose the lines of the flesh. Which is why Paul warns us in Galatians 3:2–4 (*The Message*):

How did your new life begin? Was it by working your heads off to please God? Or was it by responding to God's Message to you? Are you going to continue this craziness? For only crazy people would think they could complete by their own efforts what was begun by God. If you weren't smart enough or strong enough to begin it, how do you suppose you could perfect it? Did you go through this whole painful learning process for nothing? It is not yet a total loss, but it certainly will be if you keep this up!

So once we come to Jesus, it's about consistency—to resist the lines of this world and to pick up our lines daily and follow the Author and Finisher of our story. And when people choose to accept their lost lines from Jesus, beautiful things happen.

Finally, once we have come to Jesus and committed to living the line He gives us, we can expand our awareness of God's current activity in and around us. There is an interesting story in Genesis 28 about Jacob. On the way to his Uncle Laban's house, Jacob came to a "certain place" (v. 11) where he stopped for the night. Then he dreamed he saw a stairway to heaven with angels passing back and forth crossing the realms of heaven and earth.

Then he saw God who said to him, "I am the LORD . . . I am with you and will watch over you wherever you go . . . I will not leave you" (vv. 13, 15).

Then the text tells us:

> When Jacob awoke from his sleep, he thought, "Surely the LORD is in this place, and I was not aware of it." He was afraid and said, "How awesome is this place! This is none other than the house of God; this is the gate of heaven."
>
> —vv. 16–17

A few moments ago this was just a "certain place."

A few moments ago this was an ordinary place, a place with no name, a place to just stop for the night.

Except it wasn't.

Is God present in ordinary places? In ordinary times? In ordinary tasks?

*God is in this place, and I was not aware of it.*

God is present when we are in a worship service, but,
He is also present when we are at work, at home,
> doing the chores, taking care of the kids, watching
> television, stopping for the night someplace to
> break up a long journey.

He is present when we are cleaning dishes, reading,
> playing, driving.

We can live unaware of His presence and enter into this
> disconnect.

Jacob renamed that certain place and called it Bethel, which means "house of God." Ordinary places can turn into a house of God. Now that he had seen the presence of God there, it was no longer an ordinary place, it was no longer a place without any name, it was the house of God. God is present in this place, but we can live unaware of it.

In Jeremiah 23:24 (*The Message*), God says, "Can anyone hide out in a corner where I can't see him? . . . Am I not present everywhere, whether seen or unseen?"

Living in awareness of God and His presence is a beautiful gift God gave to the Israelites. But they often chose to live unaware of it. One time, Moses was speaking with God about the challenge of leading such a stiff-necked people. And God replied with these loving, reassuring words, "My Presence will go with you, and I will give you rest" (Exodus 33:14).

Moses then said to God, "If your Presence does not go with us, do not send us up from here. How will anyone know that you are pleased with me and with your people unless you go with us? What else will distinguish me and your people from all the other people on the face of the earth?" (vv. 15–16).

Moses not only lived in awareness of God and His presence, but he actively sought after the script of his life in every scene, every stage, and every season from God.

And God was pleased with him, "The LORD would speak to Moses face to face, as one speaks to a friend" (v. 11).

In Luke 24, we find the story of two disciples walking to Emmaus. Along the way, a man joins them and engages them in a conversation about Jesus and the events leading up to His Crucifixion and Resurrection. It is only much later that they recognize the stranger was Jesus Himself, that God was in that place, and they were not aware of it.

Your life is a sacred gift. Living in recognition of God's presence and His desire to guide, lead, and help in the here and now, in this day, today, this moment, is crucial to living out our lost lines. Abiding with Jesus during the weekdays, not just when we go to church, small groups, or during devotion time. In other words, abiding with Jesus not just in our spiritual lives but also in every aspect of our lives.

> Waking up to the voice of Jesus as revealed in His word.
> Having breakfast with Jesus.
> Getting the kids ready for school with Jesus.
> Going over the day's schedule with Jesus.
> At home, at work, at play with Jesus.
> Walking into meetings with Jesus.
> Grabbing lunch with Jesus.
> Doing laundry with Jesus.
> Vacuuming with Jesus.
> Watching the news with Jesus.
> Checking social media with Jesus.
> Cooking dinner with Jesus.
> Remaining connected to the vine,
> Drawing life-giving nutrients all day,
> Sipping living water and
> Being a source of living water for others.

We remain connected to our Line-Giver so we can receive and understand and live out our lost lines. We must allow Him full access to every part of our lives and live under His authority, His Lordship, and His direction every single day. When we do that, we start to grasp and identify and discover our lost lines.

# Chapter 12

# ZONES

There is neither Jew nor Gentile, neither slave nor free, nor is there male and female, for you are all one in Christ Jesus.

*—Galatians 3:28*

When we claim and constantly reclaim the truth of being the chosen ones, we soon discover within ourselves a deep desire to reveal to others their own chosenness. . . . That is the great joy of being chosen: the discovery that others are chosen as well. . . . There is a place for everyone—a unique, special place. Once we deeply trust that we ourselves are precious in God's eyes, we are able to recognize the preciousness of others and their unique places in God's heart.

*—Henri Nouwen,* Life of the Beloved

My wife Erika and I were at the Washington Dulles airport, getting ready to board a giant Airbus A380 on our way to India. It is the world's largest passenger airliner and can seat more than five hundred people.

Everyone was waiting in the terminal. It was early morning, which meant no one was happy. And then an airline employee picked up the microphone and said, "We will board by zones. There are six zones—A, B, C, D, E, and F. Each of you has been assigned a zone—it's on your boarding pass."

So I nudged Erika and we looked at our boarding passes. And I couldn't believe that we were assigned Zone E! People were filing in line according to their zones, and Erika and I joined the other Zone E people—we were at the back of the crowd, just one lane ahead of the unfortunate Zone F people.

Then the employee announced, "We will now board Zone A people—our first class passengers and those that have Elite Status."

So I leaned over to Erika and said, "Are we part of the elite?" And she said, "Nope." We were back of the line, bottom of the barrel people. And these elite status, first class passengers—they got up with these serious expressions on their faces, and I said to Erika, "Look at them. They will not even make eye contact with us Zone E and F people. They are the elite of our world."

They had a separate entrance. They were welcomed with a smile, a drink, a magazine, and hot towels before they laid down on their flat beds. We got nothing. We were lined up and packed like Pringles in an aluminum can.

Then we heard, "We will now board Zone B—our business class passengers." And these Zone B people, they kind of gave us surreptitious looks. Their attitude seemed to say, "You know what? We may not be Zone A, but we not Zone E or F either. It's good to be Zone B. We are on our way. Some day we will be Zone A." They would make brief eye contact and quickly look away and board the plane.

Then came Zones C and D while we Zone E and F people waited. I turned to Erika and said, "Look at all the Zone E and F people. Everyone looks so sad. No one wants to be Zone E and F, but it's right there on our boarding passes—we have been graded and grouped and assigned a Zone, and you can't change it."

They then called for Zone E. Our line started moving very slowly. There were a lot of people in Zone E and Zone F (apparently the elite status is designed in a way that very few people can get in on it). I actually felt bad for the Zone F people—they were the last of all humanity to board the plane. They looked so upset and sad and hurt. One man kept shaking his head sadly. Another woman kept sighing. They had no status, and they knew they had no status.

Actually, one young woman from Zone F held her boarding pass and tried to get with us Zone E people. But the guard was there. You are being watched. You can't just switch zones. And he saw her. And he said, "May I see your boarding pass? You are Zone F. Go to the back of the line."

And she did what any one of us would have done in the situation. She pretended like she didn't know she was Zone F! She knew. Erika and I felt so bad for her, so as soon as the guard's back was turned, we motioned to her and had her join us. She was so happy to join us Zone E people.

I was thinking about this because in our world, your lines are assigned by zones. You are either born into it or you learn very quickly which zone you belong to. There are all sorts of clubs and loyalty programs that have come up around this—I have been flying British Airways for twenty years and am part of their frequent flyer program. They have a Gold, Silver, and Bronze status for their elite members. My status is Blue. What on earth does Blue mean? It means you have no status.

You see this same separation in the workplace, in politics, and in many stories of human interaction. You see it in elementary school playgrounds and in high school cafeterias. You see it reflected by name, ethnicity, gender, nationality, and occupation. The massive relentless human tendency is to flatten individuals into neat little categories.

And it's nothing new. It has existed throughout history and in every part of the world. From ethnic divisions to racial tensions to genders, culture, and language, there are as many ways to divide people as there are people. From birth, we're handed lines that tell us which zone we're in.

But you see a pattern in the Bible. God's message is being brought to people from all backgrounds, and the unlikeliest of people hear and respond. God uses people like Gideon and Samson and Jonah and Esther.

You see this same pattern in the life of Jesus as He interacts with tax collectors, Samaritans, lepers, and the demon-possessed. People from Zone E and Zone F flocked to Him, and, amazingly, He welcomed them and they became a part of His community.

To some who were confident of their own righteousness and looked down on everyone else, Jesus told a parable.

Right at the onset, it is clear who the audience for this story was—the Zone A and Zone B people. They thought they were better than everyone else. They had elite status. And they looked down on folks who were in zones below them: "Two men went up to the temple to pray, one a Pharisee and the other a tax collector" (Luke 18:10).

It sounds like the start of a well-known joke. Two men walked into a bar—one a Republican, one a Democrat. Depending on whether you tell that joke in rural Kentucky or downtown San Francisco, everyone will know right away who's the hero and who's the villain.

Same thing here. The audience is made up of Zone A people. They know immediately the Pharisee is the hero and the tax collector is the villain. *Everyone knows that*. Pharisees were religious people; they observed all the religious rituals. They did and said the right thing. Tax collectors were sinners and cheaters and traitors.

The Pharisee stood by himself and prayed: "God, I thank you that I am not like other people—robbers, evildoers, adulterers—or even like this tax collector. I fast twice a week and give a tenth of all I get."

—vv. 11–12

The Pharisee stood by himself—He was in the elite lane. He did not walk with everyone else. He was Zone A. *He knew he was Zone A.* He was not standing with the Zone E and Zone F people. He was proud of his elite status, his Zone A card. And he reminded God how glad he was that he was not like the folks in Zone E and F, listing his credentials before God.

The people are listening and nodding. No one can touch this guy. That's a Pharisee for you. Top of the heap. Head of the list. Cream of the crop. Zone A. Elite status. But Jesus wasn't done with the story.

But the tax collector stood at a distance. He would not even look up to heaven, but beat his breast and said, "God, have mercy on me, a sinner."

—v. 13

The tax collector stood at a distance. He was Zone F. *He knew he was Zone F.* Back of the line, bottom of the barrel guy. He beat his chest. This is a common expression of deep anguish in the East. Growing up in India, I have seen people act this way in moments of extreme pain and loss. He was inconsolable.

And he was so full of remorse, he could not even look
>   up. He has heard about the name and fame of this
>   God and His power.
If God's power is not greater than his weakness,
if God's grace is not greater than his shame,
if God's promises are not greater than his past,
if God's capacity to redeem and restore is not greater
>   than the sin and disgrace of his life,
then there is absolutely no hope.
And he knows it.
He cannot even look up.

The tax collector has heard about this God and His power, holiness, and might. And all he can say is, "God, have mercy on me, a sinner." That's all he can say.

The audience nodded approvingly. Then Jesus gave the stunner of a climax.

I tell you that this man [*the Zone F guy*],
rather than the other [*the Zone A guy*], went home
justified [*loved, forgiven, redeemed*] before God.
For all those who exalt themselves will be humbled,
and those who humble themselves will be exalted.

—*v. 14*

Everyone was staring at this point. They were stunned.

I was recently at a grocery store and ran into one of our church members. I knew how he and his wife had just been through a long process of adopting a baby. He started telling me about the process, how they invested so much time and money, and it appeared the adoption agency they went through was a dubious one.

I heard his story and told him how it seemed to be that some of these adoption agencies are not just helping with adoption but are selling babies like products.

He looked at me and said, "You know what is disgusting? It's not only like products, but these products have prices attached to them based on skin, eye, and hair color. They show you this album with babies and what it'll cost to adopt them in dollar figures underneath them."

"What do you mean?" I asked. I had never heard this information before.

He said, "Do you know a baby with one kind of skin color, eye color, and gender is worth twice as much as someone of another skin color, eye color, and gender?" And I just stood there. *Who made this system?*

The lines our world hands us begin to shape and mold us and our sense of worth right from birth. That one baby is worth only half as much as another baby simply because of being born with the wrong skin color, hair color, eye color, and gender. There's actually a dollar figure attached to your name. Who made this system? Who dreamed this up?

The system God dreamed up is instead one where ultimate elite status belonged to this man named Jesus.

Philippians 2:5–8 (*The Message*) puts it this way:

> Think of yourselves the way Christ Jesus thought of himself. He had equal status with God [*Elite of the elite, Zone A++*] but didn't think so much of himself that he had to cling to the advantages of that status no matter what. Not at all. When the time came, he set aside the privileges of deity and took on the status of a slave, became human! [*He joined us Zone F people. He became*

*one of us.*] Having become human, he stayed human. It was an incredibly humbling process. He didn't claim special privileges. Instead, he lived a selfless, obedient life and then died a selfless, obedient death—and the worst kind of death at that—a crucifixion.

Jesus became like a Zone F person. He loved Zone F people—Samaritans, lepers, tax collectors, Gentiles. That made the Zone A people real mad, and they crucified Him. But on the third day, Jesus rose from the dead, defeating sin and shame. So now the barriers have been broken. And now there are neither Zone A nor Zone F, neither Jew nor Gentile, neither male nor female, but we are all one in Christ

And we come to the Cross, and all we can say is, "Please, God, have mercy on me, a sinner." Our lost lines, discovering them and living them, flows from that admission. And in this community Jesus started, there are no more sorting and grouping and grading and categorizing of people. Everyone has equal status before God. Anyone can come in. Anyone can discover their lost lines. Anyone can find love and acceptance and forgiveness.

Zone F people find out that because of Jesus, the boundaries between zones have been erased. Our lost lines allow us to shed the zoning, the categorizing, the stereotyping, the baggage of the lines we were handed. Zone A people who have had a true encounter with Jesus realize the true source of their blessings and start emulating the servant heart of Jesus. They start serving and giving and living in the way of Jesus and find it an act of unbelievable joy. And everyone realizes we have all lost our lines. We are all broken people in need of a Savior. We are all so far short of the glory of God, but we are so grateful that the gift of God is eternal life in Christ Jesus, our Lord.

As you take this journey of discovering and living your lost lines, you will have to fight the zoning. If you don't, the human zoning system will keep you conflicted. On one hand, you find your lost lines and want to live them, but on the other hand, you doubt and dither and remain divided in your commitment to live your lost lines because you can't seem to find your sense of worth and identity and status and place in God's kingdom.

So fight. First, in yourself. Do not let anyone beat you down. Because of Jesus, the zones are gone. There is no condemnation, no shaming, no guilt, no looking down on yourself. You have equal status with others before God. Second, be careful not to fall into the temptation of judging others. It can sometimes be difficult to be redeemed from being a sinful tax collector and not become a self-righteous Pharisee in the process.

*Part Three*

# THE JOURNEY

# Chapter 13

# RENEWING

So then, just as you received Christ Jesus
as Lord, continue to live your lives in him, rooted
and built up in him, strengthened in the faith as you
were taught, and overflowing with thankfulness.

—*Colossians 2:6–7*

All that is gold does not glitter,
Not all those who wander are lost;
The old that is strong does not wither,
Deep roots are not reached by the frost.
From the ashes a fire shall be woken,
A light from the shadows shall spring;
Renewed shall be blade that was broken,
The crownless again shall be king.

—*J. R. R. Tolkien*, The Fellowship of the Ring

In the first eleven chapters of Romans, Paul makes a systematic and carefully crafted presentation of the gospel. He lays out a masterful discourse on sin, forgiveness, justification, sanctification, and our identity in Christ. In essence, he walks us through the foundation of our faith.

In chapter 12, Paul pivots and offers practical guidelines of what this faith looks like. The chapter starts with this verse:

> Therefore, I urge you, brothers and sisters, in view of God's mercy, to offer your bodies as a living sacrifice, holy and pleasing to God—this is your true and proper worship.
>
> —v. 1

Simply knowing Christ and knowing theology and knowing the Bible and what it teaches us about our faith isn't enough. Our knowledge must be deeply connected with our daily living. For the fully dedicated disciple of Jesus, the knowing will spill over into doing. And the rest of the Book of Romans (except the last part) details how the gospel impacts every aspect of our lives. Total transformation will impact our bodies, our hearts, our minds, and our way of living.

Paul says we experience transformation by the renewing of our minds (v. 2). Scripture tells us the human mind is alienated from God because of sin and is depraved (Romans 1:28). The mind can entertain evil thoughts (Matthew 9:4), and in the flesh it is hostile to God (Romans 8:7), corrupted (Titus 1:15), and blinded (2 Corinthians 4:4).

The problem with our minds is that it is at war. The battle rages for our minds—lines fed to us by an enemy, by our world, by the many voices and chatter we expose ourselves to. Paul wrote earlier in Romans, "There is another power within me that is at war *with my mind*. This power makes me a slave to the sin that is still within me" (Romans 7:23 NLT, emphasis added).

Writing to the Ephesians, Paul explained it further:

> With the Lord's authority I say this: Live no longer as the Gentiles do, for they are hopelessly confused. Their minds are full of darkness; they wander far from the life God gives because they have closed their minds and hardened their hearts against him. They have no sense of shame. They live for lustful pleasure and eagerly practice every kind of impurity.
>
> —*Ephesians 4:17–19 NLT*

We discover, understand, and live our lost lines not just by ditching the ways of the world and exchanging them for a set of better rules but by the renewal of our minds.

The word for *mind* in verse 18 is used in relation to understanding, judgment, thought, state of mind, and frame of mind elsewhere in the New Testament. The idea here is that when we experience this transformation by renewal, our mindset and our very way of thinking changes.

We don't gain a new set of rules, rather we become a new person; we get a new heart and mind to live in a whole new way. The key to this new way is the renewal of our minds.

To live out our lost lines will mean living in such a way where our minds are being renewed daily, constantly, and habitually. How do we attain that? The bad news is we can't. The good news is that the Holy Spirit has the ability to do this in us.

The word translated *renewal* in our Romans 12:2 verse occurs just one other time in the New Testament:

> He saved us, not because of righteous
> things we had done, but because of his mercy.
> He saved us through the washing of rebirth and
> renewal by the Holy Spirit, whom he poured out
> on us generously through Jesus Christ our Savior.
> —*Titus 3:5–6*

Renewal by the Holy Spirit! The Holy Spirit enables us to have renewed minds. We discover and live our lost lines to the extent we are living in sync with the work of the Holy Spirit in our hearts and minds. Therefore, we must allow Him access to our minds. We must create the space for Him to work.

We do this by feeding out minds with good, nutrient-rich food. *Your mind will feed on something.* Reflect on what you listen to on the radio, what you watch on television, the constant presence of screens, and then consider how much time you spend on listening, reading, and watching things that edify your mind.

When Jesus was asked which commandment in the Law is the greatest, He replied,

> "Love the Lord your God with all your
> heart and with all your soul and with *all your
> mind.*" This is the first and greatest command-
> ment. And the second is like it: "Love your neigh-
> bor as yourself." All the Law and the Prophets
> hang on these two commandments.
> —*Matthew 22:37–40 (Emphasis added.)*

How do we do this? We start by adopting some intentional holy habits. When we adopt some holy habits, we are engaging in loving

God with all our minds and allowing the Holy Spirit to wash and renew our minds.

A few years ago, I happened to read a book on habits called *The Power of Habit*. The author, Charles Duhigg, makes a fascinating point—that our lives are mostly a collection of habits we have acquired. He develops this theme throughout that our habits can change. He claims that some habits are keystone habits. A keystone habit in one area can trigger a host of other habits or changes we may not even be aware of.

For instance, he writes, "Typically, people who exercise start eating better and becoming more productive at work. They smoke less and show more patience with colleagues and family. They use their credit cards less frequently and say they feel less stressed. . . . Exercise is a keystone habit that triggers widespread change."

He also lists how families who habitually eat dinner together seem to raise children with better homework skills, higher grades, greater emotional control, and more confidence. And here's another one—making your bed in the morning is connected to stronger skills at sticking with a budget!

As I read the book, I started thinking about what the habit of reading God's Word could potentially trigger in us. What would change if we had a habit of keeping an attitude of prayer (not necessarily long periods of prayer but an attitude of seeking God and asking His will to be done in whatever lies ahead of us)? What else would result from our discipline of fasting? Or what would attending our local church regularly and allowing our mind to be washed with worship and soaked with the words of a sermon do? Or being intentional about creating relational depth? Or putting a towel over our arms and serving? Or engaging the arts? Or practicing tithing and generosity? Or meditating? Or . . .

The problem with allowing our minds to feed on all the channels that stream a daily dose of cynicism and bad news is we gain a cynical mindset. We tune out the Holy Spirit and have trouble envisioning living our lost lines in a world full of negative buzz and distracting chatter. Paul tells us to put these things away.

> Since you have heard about Jesus and have learned the truth that comes from him, throw off your old sinful nature and your former way of life, which is corrupted by lust and deception. Instead, *let the Spirit renew your thoughts and attitudes.* Put on your new nature, created to be like God—truly righteous and holy.
> —*Ephesians 4:21–24 NLT (Emphasis added.)*

But what does it mean to let the Spirit renew our thoughts and attitudes? Paul lists the kind of things we should be feeding our minds on:

> Whatever is true, whatever is noble, whatever is right, whatever is pure, whatever is lovely, whatever is admirable—if anything is excellent or praiseworthy—*think about such things.*
> —*Philippians 4:8 (Emphasis added.)*

Which is why feeding your mind on the Word of God is
    so extremely important,
why listening to edifying songs is so valuable,
why going to church and being part of a community to
    encourage one another is so vital,
why reading good books that build your faith is so
    significant,

why the company of saints is so crucial,

why praying is so necessary,

why serving and giving and worshipping is so essential.

These are all ways you allow the Holy Spirit space and time to renew your mind. The Bible makes it clear that in Christ, we have received the Holy Spirit who enables us to understand what God has given us, revealed to us, and wants us to do. In essence, *we have the mind of Christ* (1 Corinthians 2:16).

The mind of Christ!

This is explosive news! To have the mind of Christ means we can no longer look at ourselves, our lives, and our days the same way. Our lives become shaped by our overriding, overwhelming, overarching mission—"If Jesus was in my place right now . . ." Every decision, every interaction, every word, every thought, every action is now pulsating with the potential of being in harmony with our lost lines.

Having the mind of Christ means we think like Jesus
would in our situation.

We react and respond like Jesus.

We feel what Jesus would feel.

We detest the things Jesus detests.

We are drawn to the things Jesus is drawn to.

Our hearts are broken by the things that break the heart
of Jesus.

We join Jesus in bringing hope to the hopeless.

We live with Jesus-inspired levels of generosity,
gratitude, and humility.

We exchange mindless consumption for godly
contentment.

With the eyes of Jesus, we see the church in a whole new
　　way—as the radiant, shining, shimmering bride of
　　Christ.
We relate like Jesus,
we think like Jesus,
we speak like Jesus,
we act like Jesus,
we serve like Jesus,
we give like Jesus.
We join in and enthusiastically pray like Jesus did—that
　　God's will would be done and His kingdom would
　　come on earth as it is in heaven.

We live as one whose mind is like Jesus' not with a sense of
obligation but because our hearts and minds are so in the grip of
the Holy Spirit that *we cannot not do it*. We follow the rhythm of a
different dynamic, a different reality, a different way of living.

It means we start each day with this central conviction—

I no longer live, but Christ lives in me.
　　　　　　　　　　　　　　　　　—*Galatians 2:20*

And Paul says when we live this way, we will discern the will of God,
which is good and pleasing and perfect (Romans 12:2). In essence,
when we live this way, we discover and live our lost lines.

# Chapter 14

# CONNECT

This is the confidence we have in approaching God: that if we ask anything according to his will, he hears us.

*—1 John 5:14*

No nobler reply ever fell from the lips of [a] ruler, than that uttered by President Lincoln in response to the clergyman who ventured to say, in his presence, that he hoped "the Lord was on our side." "I am not at all concerned about that," replied Mr. Lincoln, "for I know that the Lord is always on the side of the right. But it is my constant anxiety and prayer that I and this nation should be on the Lord's side."

*—Francis Bicknell Carpenter,*
Six Months at the White House with Abraham Lincoln

There is a term in technology called *ambient awareness*. There are several different definitions of it, but in its simplest form, ambient awareness is the connection or awareness created between two people who may not be physically present next to each other. Social networking apps like Facebook, Skype, and Twitter are examples of ways one can experience and live in ambient awareness of one's loved ones and friends.

In his *The New York Times* article "Brave New World of Digital Intimacy," Clive Thompson describes ambient awareness as something "very much like being physically near someone and picking up on his mood through the little things he does—body language, sighs, stray comments—out of the corner of your eye." It describes the connection two people can feel when they make the effort to stay in touch even when they cannot physically see each other. The more they learn about each other, the more they keep the dialogue going, keep in touch with common friends in a community of social media, and check in on each other. The relationship, which otherwise would have dried up and faded, is revitalized and strengthened on an ongoing basis.

Thompson says, "Each little update—each individual bit of social information—is insignificant on its own, even supremely mundane. But taken together, over time, the little snippets coalesce into a surprisingly sophisticated portrait of your friends' and family members' lives, like thousands of dots making a pointillist painting."

It is well known that social media has some severe limits, and it of course cannot take the place of real relationships and community. But when I first read about ambient awareness, it resonated with me. I have family and friends around the world, and to be able to pick up my phone and connect with them through WhatsApp and get a response within seconds is not only amazing, but the cumulative effect is that through many birthdays and births and milestones and sickness and sorrow and joy and prayer requests, there has been a relational depth that otherwise would not have been possible. To live in ambient awareness of a friend or someone you love and to be able to constantly and relationally connect with that person you cannot see personally is a gift.

We have been given a greater gift of living in ambient awareness of our Line-Giver—to be able to instantly and in real-time be able to connect, communicate, and live in intimate community with Him. That awesome, holy, and powerful gift is the gift of prayer.

Author and evangelist Leonard Ravenhill writes in his book *Why Revival Matters*:

> **No man is greater than his prayer life. The pastor who is not praying is playing; the people who are not praying are straying. . . . We have many organizers, but few agonizers; many players and payers, few pray-ers; many singers, few clingers . . . many fears, few tears; much fashion, little passion; many interferers, few intercessors; many writers, but few fighters. If we fail here, we fail everywhere.**

A little convicting, isn't it?

The Bible tells us to pray continually (1 Thessalonians 5:17). In every situation, by prayer and petition, with thanksgiving, we should present our requests to God (Philippians 4:6). If we ask anything according to God's will, He hears us (1 John 5:14), and where two or three are gathered, Jesus is there (Matthew 18:20). God's house, the church, is called a house of prayer (Isaiah 56:7). Prayer is so important because it is the most powerful tool we have been given to discover and live our lost lines.

Prayer, quite simply, is connecting with God and living in ambient awareness of Him. It can take the form of words, silence, or worship and can include praise, confession, adoration, intercession, and so on. At its core, prayer is connecting with God.

The disciples noticed prayer was important to Jesus. Jesus lived a full and abundant life. He certainly had a lot of things to do, but He also lived a life saturated with prayer. Jesus prayed, and He prayed often. He lived in daily ambient awareness of God. He healed people through prayer. He prayed before making important decisions. He prayed when a problem arose. He was praying when the Holy Spirit descended on Him. He prayed over children. He prayed alone and with others. He prayed short and long prayers. He prayed in thanksgiving and in moments of anguish.

The disciples saw how Jesus prayed, and they saw how Jesus lived with a deep abiding sense of love and joy and peace. They wanted to live in ambient awareness of God like Jesus. So one day they came to Jesus and said, "Lord, teach us to pray" (Luke 11:1).

So Jesus did. We call that prayer the Lord's Prayer, and it is a model for how we should pray. An incident that happened between my thirteen-year-old daughter Ashlynne and me reminded me in a small way of the significance of the Lord's Prayer.

Ashlynne had been working on our family computer, which is kept in the living room. She stepped away for a few minutes, and I saw she had left the browser on with her email account. She was not around, and now I had access to her email! So I sat down, and in one sense, hacked into her email and wrote an email to myself from her. This is what I wrote:

Hi Dad,

You are really cool. I love making tea for you and mom.

Your loving daughter,
Ashlynne

(She had recently learned to make Indian tea for her mom and me.) Then I logged into my email and replied to the email I wrote to myself from her. And this is what I wrote:

Thanks, Ashlynne. We love having you make tea for us.

I love you,
Dad

The next day, I got a response from her that said:

Wait, WHAT??? When did I write that???

A few moments later, she wrote another email saying:

No, wait. You wrote it from my email than emailed "me" back. That's real great, Dad.

And it struck me. God did the same thing to us. He created us, loves us, and wants to relate to us. He wants us to communicate with Him, and He wants us to find and live our lost lines. And in Jesus, God hacked into humanity and then in the Lord's Prayer, *God is writing an email, a communication, a prayer to Himself from us.*

Incredible, isn't it?

God is now here. And He is teaching us to how to live in ambient awareness of Him so we can discover and live the lost lines we were meant to live! So, let's walk through this prayer, which is a model set forth by Jesus on how we can live in ambient awareness of God and therefore rise above the chatter of this world. The more we communicate with Him, the better we'll be able to at any moment and in any circumstance, discover and live our lost lines.

Jesus started the prayer this way:

Our Father in Heaven, hallowed be Your name.

—*v. 2 NKJV*

It all starts by first understanding who our Line-Giver is—our Father. To the listeners, this would have been remarkable. No one referred to God as father before. To a Middle Eastern audience, the idea of God as father means He is someone who will protect and provide. He is someone who can be trusted. We who are in Christ have access to the Line-Giver as our Father in any moment. Even if we cannot physically see Him, we can live in ambient awareness of Him.

> He is our Father.
> He is your Father.
> He made you.
> He designed you with a purpose and a plan.
> He wants to have a strong and unending relationship
>     with you.
> He will never betray you or abandon you.
> He wants you to get to know your brothers and sisters
>     that are all part of His family.
> He will forgive you.
> He will guide you.
> He will cause all things to work out for good for you if
>     you place your trust in Him.
> And the more you talk to Him and get to know Him, the
>     easier it will be to live in ambient awareness of Him.

To hallow God's name is to give Him the place in your life He deserves—above all else. It means recognizing His holiness, His power, His presence, His sovereignty, His righteousness, His love, justice, mercy, and faithfulness. It means giving Him the worship and adoration He so richly deserves.

If we want to live in awareness of God in our world, we start by first defining our relationship with Him, our Line-Giver. The fact that He is our Father sets a foundation of security for us on which everything else stands.

**Your kingdom come. Your will be done on earth as it is in Heaven.**

*—v. 2 NKJV*

All throughout the Gospels, the good news is presented as the coming of the kingdom of God because of Jesus. God's rule has now begun. And so the disciples are to pray that the kingdom of God will continue to grow and expand and come to its fullness. It orients us to a different reality. It makes us aware of the fact that we are now citizens of a different kingdom and we live by different rules. Our lost lines are part of the grand story of God's kingdom coming to earth.

**Give us each day our daily bread.**

*—v. 3*

We recognize that all good things we have and are blessed with ultimately come from our Father (James 1:17). Living our lost lines means living with the awareness that our Line-Giver has given us everything we need to live out our lost lines.

It is interesting that Jesus uses the word *daily*. Praying then is living in recognition of daily reliance on God. Every single day, like the Israelites receiving manna in the desert, we are to live with this awareness of God's provision.

**And forgive us our sins, for we also forgive everyone who is indebted to us.**

*—Luke 11:4 NKJV*

Lewis Smedes writes in *Forgive and Forget*, "When we forgive, we set a prisoner free and then discover that the prisoner we set free was us."

Forgiveness is not minimizing, denying, enabling, or brushing aside the wrong, hurt, or pain. It does not mean staying in an abusive situation. It does not always lead to reconciliation or restore broken trust. It does not mean the person will not face legal consequences for a crime. It means you personally give up the right to get even. You release the debt to God and allow healing to begin in your heart. And you do it because you live in God's generosity toward you.

> Because God has been so generous to us,
> because He has given us everything we need,
> because He has forgiven us the unpayable debt of sin we
>     owed,
> we now extend that same posture to others.
> We don't extend forgiveness to receive forgiveness.
> We have received forgiveness so we can extend
>     forgiveness.

**And do not lead us not into temptation, but deliver us from the evil one.**

— *v. 4 NKJV*

If you are tempted to veer from your lost lines, it's a good idea to immerse yourself in prayer and Scripture and call someone you can talk to. Don't try to face it alone. Veering off course can have profound consequences—people have sacrificed their integrity, destroyed their families, lost their bond to a community, and been driven to isolation and despair.

Living our lost lines in this world means we are constantly a target for an enemy who tempts us to abandon our mission. But our Line-Giver is ever present to help us not succumb to it. And in those moments when trials come and the lines get tough to live, the promise is that He will walk with us through it. He will see us through.

For Yours is the kingdom and the power and the glory forever. Amen.

—*Matthew 6:13*

The prayer ends with a fitting doxology reminding us all that ultimately the Author of the story of our lives is God. His is the story, the kingdom, the power, and the glory. We are privileged to be able to play a part in it.

You will notice all the pronouns in this prayer are plural. There is a collective posture to this prayer. That's intentional. The personal for Jesus finds meaning in the community. God is my Father, but He is also our Father. We may pray in solitude, but we never pray alone. We pray with others and the Holy Spirit. The plural pronouns remind us we belong to a great big family of God. Our lost lines are to be lived with others who are also living out their lost lines. When we all live out our parts, the great kingdom story comes together as God's magnum opus, a mesmerizing and irresistible narrative that beckons all who see it to discover, find, and live out their lost lines as well.

Prayer (and the Lord's Prayer) is a great way to remain connected to our Line-Giver no matter where we are, what we are doing, or what we are facing. We can call on Him, draw on Him, and seek His assistance at any time.

To live our lost lines, to be able to thwart the voices that pull us to conform to the patterns of our world, to allow the Holy Spirit to renew our minds and be able to discern the will of God, we will need to live in ambient awareness of our Line-Giver. To keep sending updates in real time. To keep connecting and posting and communicating throughout the day. To invoke His presence and His wisdom and His strength and His guidance in all that we think, say, and do. And His beautiful promise is that He will be with us always, even until the end of the age (Matthew 28:20).

# Chapter 15

# ENSEMBLE

After this I looked, and there before me was a great multitude that no one could count, from every nation, tribe, people and language, standing before the throne and before the Lamb. They were wearing white robes and were holding palm branches in their hands. And they cried out in a loud voice: "Salvation belongs to our God, who sits on the throne, and to the Lamb."

—*Revelation 7:9–10*

The more genuine and the deeper our community becomes, the more will everything else between us recede, the more clearly and purely will Jesus Christ and His work become the one and only thing that is vital between us.

—*Dietrich Bonhoeffer*, Life Together

In 2016, a reporter from the travel magazine *Afar* wrote an article titled, "The Incredibly True Story of Renting a Friend in Tokyo." People work hard and long hours, they have a lot to do, and there isn't any time for friendship. Enter Client

Partners, an agency that can provide you with a fake but warm and gentle friend to talk to at a café or a restaurant for a short period of time. The reporter rented a friend for a couple hours and detailed his experience having dinner and a stroll down the streets of Tokyo with his rented friend.

The reporter then decided to talk to Maki Abe, the CEO of Client Partners, the largest agency of its kind in Japan. She explained, "We look like a rich country from the outside . . . So many people are alone with their problems, and stuck, and their hearts aren't touching."

*Their hearts aren't touching!*

The lines the world hands us keep many of us stuck, alone, lonely, and for so many people, the reality is that their hearts aren't touching. Writing more than twenty-five years ago, author Rollo May argued in his book *The Cry for Myth* that of all the myths in America, none was more potent than the myth of the Wild West. So many heroes like Kit Carson, Annie Oakley, and Butch Cassidy and the Sundance Kid came out of this myth, and the overarching archetype that emerged was that of the brave and fearless cowboy who lived alone and then bragged about it. May argues this myth won the admiration of Americans everywhere. To be able to stand alone in freedom and courage and be self-sufficient led to the notion of rugged individualism, in which "each individual must learn to take care of himself or herself and thus be beholden to no one else."

But, May passionately contends, this aspiration for rugged individualism robbed Americans of any solid community of their own. He lists a litany of traits rugged individualism engendered— narcissistic personalities, loneliness, a focus on the self above everything else, depression, fear and anxiety, a country of citizens with many acquaintances but no close friends, and a life that is "exasperatingly empty." Our hearts aren't touching.

When God created the heavens and the earth, the earth was without form, empty and dark. God then created day and night, land and water, sea creatures and land creatures, birds and vegetation. And at every stage of this extravagant creative act, God looked at what He had done, and the text tells us that God saw it was good.

There is, however, one place in the perfect world of Genesis 1–2, where the text tells us God saw something and said it was not good, "The LORD God said, 'It is not good for the man to be alone. I will make a helper suitable for him'" (Genesis 2:18).

Being alone is not good. Being lonely is not good. Trying to live your life by yourself is not good. We were created and designed and meant to live our lost lines within the context of a community. This theme is repeated throughout Scripture from Genesis to Revelation.

One fundamental thing to remember on your journey to living your lost lines is that your lost lines are not really about you, and you cannot live your lost lines without others. Our lost lines are part of the greater story.

First, it is important to understand that our Line-Giver started this community called the church. It is the ensemble that includes all those who have received and are now living out their lost lines. The church has been a part of His plan from the beginning—to create a community of people committed to Him who He can bless and guide and lead and then make a conduit of blessing, a channel for others to learn and receive their lost lines. He is the Author of our lost lines, He is the Designer of this ensemble, He is the Sustainer of His community, and He is its most glorious and important inhabitant cast member.

Which is why our Line-Giver is present in a very special way in this ensemble. Right before He ascended, Jesus gave these instructions to the ensemble:

God authorized and commanded me to commission you: Go out and train everyone you meet, far and near, in this way of life, marking them by baptism in the threefold name: Father, Son, and Holy Spirit. Then instruct them in the practice of all I have commanded you. I'll be with you as you do this, day after day after day, right up to the end of the age.

—*Matthew 28:18–20 The Message*

Jesus is present within His community in a very special way. Another time, Jesus tells His disciples, "For where two or three gather in my name, there am I with them" (Matthew 18:20).

The Line-Giver is always here and always present, but He is present with us in the context of His community in a unique and special way. When we gather in *His* name, supernatural things happen. We start to experience transformation of hearts and renewal of minds and discernment of His good and perfect will. The author of Hebrews illustrates that when we do this, when we live in community and in obedience to our Line-Giver, we discover and live our lost lines in ways we could not if we tried alone.

So let's do it—full of belief, confident that we're presentable inside and out. Let's keep a firm grip on the promises that keep us going. He always keeps his word. Let's see how inventive we can be in encouraging love and helping out, not avoiding worshiping together as some do but spurring each other on, especially as we see the big Day approaching.

—*Hebrews 10:22–25 The Message*

This spurring, encouraging, and cheering on as we live our lost lines is unique to the ensemble of our Line-Giver. It is the way of God. Solomon writes in Ecclesiastes 4:9 (NLT), "Two people are better off than one, for they can help each other succeed."

In the ensemble of the Line-Giver, we not only receive and live out our lost lines, we do it in community with others. We encourage each other and know that our Line-Giver is present in a unique and special way in our midst.

Second, in this ensemble, everyone has a role, a part. When we live out our lost lines, we are not only fulfilling our story, but we are living out our story as part of the larger story. Which is why when one person doesn't take ownership of their lines, the story remains sort of incomplete.

Which also means that in this ensemble, no one has a supersized role. This script is not like a Hollywood script. Apart from the role of our Line-Giver, there are no superstar roles. God designed it this way. There are no big or small roles in God's story. Every role, every person, is of equal importance. The guy behind the pulpit is doing just as important of a job as the person serving coffee at the hospitality center or the woman planting flowers in her neighbor's yard or the dad serving with his kids at a rescue mission.

Those who seem to have lead parts can't tell the ones who seem to have supporting roles that their parts are somehow less important. All roles are important, essential, and critical, and when everyone does their part really well, the story of God emerges in a beautiful, winsome, captivating, engaging, and delightful way.

Third, the defining characteristic of this ensemble of people finding and living their lost lines is a deep love for God and each other. Our Line-Giver repeatedly said to love one another. One time, He went so far as to say that people outside this community would look in and know we are part of the Line-Giver's ensemble because of the way we love each other (John 13:34–35).

Our Line-Giver desires for us to live out our lost lines from the foundation of His love, which would impact the way we treat one another. The Bible talks about this a lot:

Honor one another.

—*Romans 12:10*

Live in harmony with one another.

—*Romans 12:16*

Accept one another, then, just as Christ accepted you.

—*Romans 15:7*

Encourage one another.

—*2 Corinthians 13:11*

Serve one another humbly in love.

—*Galatians 5:13*

Be patient, bearing with one another in love.

—*Ephesians 4:2*

Be kind and compassionate to one another.

—*Ephesians 4:32*

Bear with each other and forgive one another.

—*Colossians 3:13*

Offer hospitality to one another.

—*1 Peter 4:9*

Clothe yourselves with humility toward one another.

—*1 Peter 5:5*

These are the hallmarks of the ensemble that is living out their lost lines.

In one of the most profound prayers of Jesus recorded in the Bible, Jesus said:

My prayer is not for them alone. I pray also for those who will believe in me through their message, that all of them may be one, Father, just as you are in me and I am in you. May they also be in us so that the world may believe that you have sent me. I have given them the glory that you gave me, that they may be one as we are one—I in them and you in me—so that they may be brought to complete unity. Then the world will know that you sent me and have loved them even as you have loved me.

—*John 17:20–23*

The theme of this deep sense of love and community is at the heart of the ensemble Jesus put in place for the world to find and live their lost lines. A place where our hearts are touching, connecting, and resonating with each other and that of our Line-Giver.

The whole reason for this ensemble is to get the news out that "Christ died for our sins according to the Scriptures, that he was buried, that he was raised on the third day according to the Scriptures" (1 Corinthians 15:3–4). Paul, writing in Colossians 1:28–29 (CEV), makes it clear why he worked so hard—"We announce the message about Christ, and we use all our wisdom to warn and teach everyone, so that all of Christ's followers will grow and become mature. That's why I work so hard and use the mighty power he gives me."

The goal of this ensemble is to announce the message of Christ and help each member find their lost lines and grow and mature in living them out. God meant for us to live our lives in ways where our hearts touch other hearts and lead them to finding and living their lost lines.

The Bible records that there was once such an ensemble. A community of Christ that proclaimed Him fearlessly, facing impossible odds, and the Holy Spirit moved in a powerful way. They would teach and learn, pray and break bread, and lived in unity and fellowship. They lived with their masks off. They single-mindedly searched and found and lived their lost lines. They walked closely with the Line-Giver, spurred one another to do good works that God had planned for them to do, gave sacrificially, served joyfully, and loved selflessly.

They took bold risks, and things didn't always go smoothly. They faced conflict, things got messy, and they were persecuted. But they had tasted what it was like to find and live their lost lines. Their hearts were ignited by a vision of a future where there would be no more tears and no more pain and no more death. That our

Line-Giver is coming back and He would restore everything the way it was in Genesis and He would dwell with His people.

And our world has never been the same. In a world where there is so much darkness, so many divisions, so much violence and hurt and pain, what if once again, the ensemble of Jesus rose up, gripped by the power of the Holy Spirit, and were passionate about finding and living their lost lines, living in fearless obedience to the Line-Giver, walking in unity and fellowship and prayer and breaking of bread, giving sacrificially, serving joyfully, and loving selflessly?

There are millions of us who have caught hold of the vision our Line-Giver has entrusted to us. And we are motivated by a different vision, our ears tuned to a different song, our hearts beating in rhythm with the heart of our Line-Giver. Millions of miniensembles of every kind, color, and culture in every nation, every tribe, every language—one unifying goal—to proclaim Christ and to help people find their lost lines and grow and mature in living them out. A vision of life and community that doesn't end at death's door but goes right past it into eternity.

Any other vision is a downgrade for your life.

# Chapter 16

# RETAKES

You, Lord, are forgiving and good,
abounding in love to all who call to you.

—*Psalm 86:5*

To say that God turns away from the
wicked is like saying that the sun hides from the
blind.

—*Saint Anthony the Great*

As we discover and live out our lost lines, it is important to note at the outset that there is a distinct possibility you will mess up a scene! Many heroes of the faith did too. There are a number of ways a misstep can occur.

First, we may discover our lost lines but decide not to intentionally live them out. A prophet named Jonah did just that. His story begins this way:

The word of the Lord came to Jonah
son of Amittai: "Go to the great city of Nineveh
and preach against it, because its wickedness has
come up before me."

—*Jonah 1:1–2*

No one said finding and living your lost lines promises a life of ease and convenience. Nineveh was the capital of a violent, cruel, wicked, and ruthless country. And the Line-Giver tells Jonah he is to go into this violent, cruel, wicked, and ruthless country and *preach against it*. Nineveh is a place marked with fear, danger, and uncertainty. Sometimes our lost lines will take us way out of our comfort zone.

> But Jonah ran away from the LORD and headed for Tarshish. He went down to Joppa, where he found a ship bound for that port. After paying the fare, he went aboard and sailed for Tarshish to flee from the LORD.
>
> —v. 3

Jonah ran in the opposite direction from the wicked evil city of Nineveh to the wealthy, prosperous town of Tarshish. And you likely know the rest of the story. God sent a huge storm, and the sailors were afraid. They eventually threw Jonah into the sea, the storms calmed down, and Jonah was swallowed by a large fish. This is not your everyday prophet story.

So what happens when you receive your lost lines and decide to shut God out and run, literally or metaphorically, in the opposite direction? Chances are, you will hit a storm. But what looks like a bad thing can turn out to be a good thing. When we receive our lost lines and intentionally decide to not live them out, the Line-Giver, who is watching what we are doing all along, will allow us to hit a wall. And when you hit a wall, everything slows down.

And so it was with Jonah. He is in a desperate situation—no more hiding, no more running, no more avoiding the Line-Giver. And he discovers something powerful about the Line-Giver . . . we'll get into that in a moment. All of Jonah 2 is a desperate, honest, and authentic prayer.

In my distress I called to the LORD, and he answered me. From deep in the realm of the dead I called for help, and you listened to my cry. . . . I said, "I have been banished from your sight; yet I will look again toward your holy temple." The engulfing waters threatened me, the deep surrounded me; seaweed was wrapped around my head. To the roots of the mountains I sank down; the earth beneath barred me in forever. But you, LORD my God, brought my life up from the pit. When my life was ebbing away, I remembered you, LORD, and my prayer rose to you, to your holy temple.

*—Jonah 2:1–7*

And God commanded the fish, and it vomited Jonah out on land. Jonah 1 is about Jonah discovering his lost lines and intentionally not living them out. Jonah 2 is when Jonah hits a wall and turns back to the Line-Giver. To get to chapter 3 of the story, Jonah will have to get through chapter 2 of confession and repentance. Notice the way chapter 3 begins, "Then the word of the LORD came to Jonah a second time: 'Go to the great city of Nineveh and proclaim to it the message I give you'" (vv. 1–2).

Chapter 3 begins the same way chapter 1 does! The Line-Giver's plans haven't changed. He hasn't given up on Jonah (or the Ninevites). Jonah discovers that he is allowed a retake!

When we disobey and run and act out of fear or insecurity and hit a wall, our Line-Giver allows us retakes *if we turn to Him.* The point about Jonah is that when he hit a wall, he turned to his Line-Giver. He understood it is actually a lot safer to live his lost lines in the dangerous city of Nineveh than follow the lines of this world in the prosperous city of Tarshish. And when he did, when he repented and turned back to his Line-Giver, he found out that the Line-Giver allows retakes.

The second way we can flub our lines is through sin. The story of the Bible is one long list of people who had ups and downs in their journey to living out their lost lines. There was Abraham whose lost lines included the birth of a promised son. But Abraham had a son out of wedlock in his attempt to help God along. There was Moses who murdered a man. There was David, a man after God's own heart, who committed adultery. In the New Testament, we find Peter, who denied our Lord in an epic display of public failure.

And in each case, they turned to the Line-Giver, and He allowed them retakes. Maybe the current scene in the story of your life is a particularly awful one. Maybe you are thinking you have flubbed your lines so badly there is simply no hope.

There was once a king named Manasseh. He indulged in sin and evil. He renounced God, built altars to idols, sacrificed his children to these idols, and practiced witchcraft. The Bible tells us that "Manasseh led Judah and the people of Jerusalem astray, so that they did more evil than the nations the LORD had destroyed before the Israelites" (2 Chronicles 33:9).

His actions led to the country being invaded, and he was taken a prisoner. Manasseh then reflected on all he had done. He hit a wall. He deeply repented of his ways and turned to the Line-Giver. And his story began to change.

And when he prayed to him, the LORD was moved by his entreaty and listened to his plea; so he brought him back to Jerusalem and to his kingdom. Then Manasseh knew that the LORD is God.

—v. 13

There's always hope. The only person who doesn't have hope is the one who refuses to repent and find his or her way back. No excuses, no rationalization, no justifications. Just coming to our Line-Giver and throwing ourselves at His mercy and grace.

Likewise, when David was confronted about his affair, he didn't try to offer any pretexts. Rather, he responded:

> Have mercy on me, O God, according to your unfailing love; according to your great compassion blot out my transgressions. Wash away all my iniquity and cleanse me from my sin. . . . Against you, you only, have I sinned and done what is evil in your sight; so you are right in your verdict and justified when you judge. Surely I was sinful at birth, sinful from the time my mother conceived me. Yet you desired faithfulness even in the womb; you taught me wisdom in that secret place. Cleanse me with hyssop, and I will be clean; wash me, and I will be whiter than snow. Let me hear joy and gladness; let the bones you have crushed rejoice. . . . Create in me a pure heart, O God, and renew a steadfast spirit within me. Do not cast me from your presence or take your Holy Spirit from me. Restore to me the joy of your salvation and grant me a willing spirit, to sustain me.
>
> —*Psalm 51:1–12*

John asserts this by saying, "If we claim to be without sin, we deceive ourselves and the truth is not in us. If we confess our sins, he is faithful and just and will forgive us our sins and purify us from all unrighteousness" (1 John 1:8–9).

Grace is available. Forgiveness is available. A new start is available. You can start by turning to the Line-Giver and confess and seek to be restored by His power and mercy.

It is important to note that the consequences of our sin and action don't always go away. Sometimes the hurt and the pain and the devastation we may have caused remains and has to be dealt with. David, Jonah, and Manasseh all struggled with the consequences of their actions. But the Line-Giver offered them retakes in response to their confession and genuine repentance.

Truth is, we all have our mess. And that's part of our story, our narrative, our message. I was looking at the word *message* and suddenly realized it is made up of two words: *mess* plus *age*!

Yes, there are times when you will flub the lines.

But you don't give up.

Here's the deal—God allows retakes. The thing to remember is that you can't move to the next scene, the next part of your story, until you get this part right. The good news is that if we come to him and repent of our sins, He is faithful and just and will forgive us our sins and purify us from all unrighteousness. That's His promise.

Third, the way to get better at living our lost lines is to realize that this struggle is real and try not to focus on the wrong thing. Paul wrote about this quite clearly. I want to share *The Message* translation of this familiar passage with you:

What I don't understand about myself is that I decide one way, but then I act another, doing things I absolutely despise. So if I can't be trusted to figure out what is best for myself and then do it, it becomes obvious that God's command is necessary. But I need something more! For if I know the law but still can't keep it, and if the power of sin within me keeps sabotaging my best intentions, I obviously need help! I realize that I don't have what it takes. I can will it, but I can't do it. I decide to do good, but I don't really do it; I decide not to do bad, but then I do it anyway. My decisions, such as they are, don't result in actions. Something has gone wrong deep within me and gets the better of me every time. . . . I've tried everything and nothing helps. I'm at the end of my rope. Is there no one who can do anything for me? Isn't that the real question? The answer, thank God, is that Jesus Christ can and does. He acted to set things right in this life of contradictions where I want to serve God with all my heart and mind, but am pulled by the influence of sin to do something totally different.

—*Romans 7:15–25 The Message*

To get to chapter 3 of the story, you will have to get through chapter 2. The point is not to try harder and harder to avoid living the lines of this world. You will feel exhausted and defeated and beaten down trying to win that game. The joy will be sucked out of you. You will find yourself trapped in legalism. You are not your maker. Therefore you are not your line-giver. Trying to control and take care of your sin and rebellion and disobedience in your own efforts is a fool's errand.

The point is to learn as much as you can about our Line-Giver, to walk closely with Him and to actively ask, seek, knock, and discover your lost lines—to keep your mind focused on finding and living your lost lines. The more you focus your attention and your life on God's lines for you, the more you will know that your identity and your future and your very life for all of eternity is secure in His hands. He is at work in you. And no matter what, you can always turn to Him. So you turn your heart, your mind, your will, your decisions, and your life to Him. There's true, deep, unshakeable love there. There's joy there. There's freedom there.

# ENDURING

Chapter 17

So do not fear, for I am with you; do not be dismayed, for I am your God. I will strengthen you and help you; I will uphold you with my righteous right hand.

—Isaiah 41:10

It's like driving a car at night. You never see further than your headlights, but you can make the whole trip that way.

—E. L. Doctorow

In our journey in living out our lost lines, there will be stretches when we will be called to seasons of endurance. The sun will hide behind the clouds, darkness will seem to overtake the light, and the storm will threaten to sink our boat. Part of our struggle in this is not knowing every scene, every part of our lost lines.

We need to know God often does not reveal the next scene in our individual stories until we have lived the current one well. God doesn't tell Abraham right away what He plans to do. He gives him his lost lines. Abraham knows God's grand plan is to bless him and to make him a channel of blessing to others. But the lines Abraham gets only contain the next scene: "Go from your country, your people and your father's household to the land I will show you" (Genesis 12:1).

Abraham has to master that scene before God will reveal to him the next scene. Without him leaving his country and his people and going to the land God was going to show him, the next scene cannot be played out.

There are many reasons God reveals his plan bits at a time. If God revealed His entire plan to us, we could very well be overwhelmed. He wants to grow our character, our faith, and our decision-making skills. Along the way, He knows we'll most likely need to take some retakes. And then there are scenes that involve pain and trials and tests that could crush us. God, in His mercy, often reveals what we need to know to live our current scene.

In the Book of Acts, when Paul encounters Jesus, Jesus doesn't give him the lost lines of his entire life. Jesus simply tells him the next scene: "I want you to get up and enter the city. In the city you'll be told what to do next" (Acts 9:6 *The Message*).

This is often true of us. The truth is, live long enough and you *will* face scenes of massive storms and profound sorrows and intense pain. And yet, Scripture tells us it is in these moments that deep faith-forging, soul-shaping, character-forming work is going on, "We rejoice in our sufferings, knowing that suffering produces endurance, and endurance produces character, and character produces hope" (Romans 5:3–4 ESV).

The promise is that if you walk closely with the Author of your lost lines, you will never lose hope. Where does this hope come from?

**And hope does not put us to shame, because God's love has been poured into our hearts through the Holy Spirit who has been given to us.**

*—v. 5 ESV*

In those moments of pain and suffering and testing and trials, it may seem as though you have lost your lost lines. It may seem as though the Author of your lost lines has taken them back and left you on your own. It may seem as though you are living the last scene of your story. It may seem as though you will never make it past this scene.

As a pastor, I see many people going through some very tough situations. I see the dozens and dozens of prayer requests we get each week—for marriages on the brink, rebellious children, crushing financial issues, addiction challenges, divorce, illnesses, sheer exhaustion, loneliness, lots of fear, and anxiety. I see it every week.

And the difficulty we have is there are times when our Line-Giver seems so distant, disengaged, and disinterested, despite many prayers. And we wonder if we will ever get to live our lost lines. Or if we even have the right lines.

In my thirty-plus years as a Christian, I have gone through many such moments. And the most recent one happened last year. I had my left thyroid removed because of a nodule that turned out to be benign. Before the surgery, I was told there was a 0.27 percent chance of a complication that could impact my voice. A rarer complication could completely alter or reduce the capacity of my voice. Given that I work as a pastor and preacher, this was a sobering complication to consider. After much prayer and discussion with family and friends, I decided to go ahead with the surgery.

An hour after surgery, the diagnosis came. My vocal cords were completely unresponsive. I could not utter a single word. When I tried to speak, only a hoarse indistinct whoosh came out. Over the next day, a team of medical personnel ran numerous tests. They were stumped. And then the doctor stood by my bed and painted three scenarios. I still remember his closing words, "Mr. Pillai, worst-case scenario—you may never regain your voice."

I remember thinking, *This is just surreal.* My wife Erika, who was sitting next to me holding my hand, burst into tears.

What do you do when you are a preacher and the surgeon looks at you and says you may never speak again?

What do you do when your world goes silent?

What do you do when you can no longer speak to the woman you love and the daughters you adore?

What do you do when you are a pastor and cannot even meet people because you are now mute?

The medical team decided to let me go home and wait for a week to see if there would be any natural rejuvenation of the vocal cords. My next appointment was in eight days. For the next eight days, I could not speak a single word. I knew our elders and friends and folks at our church and circle were diligently praying. There were people who fasted and prayed. My four girls prayed such beautiful prayers over me.

But no voice. I couldn't do the things I normally did. I could not meet people. When the phone rang, I couldn't answer it. I couldn't go to the grocery store. I couldn't even go out. I was using slate and chalk to communicate with my family. I realized how precious the gift of voice was.

I dug into Scripture, and I learned a few things about living my lost lines when your world crashes around you. The first set of insights came from David. In chapter 7, I talked about David's heart. There was something else about David that helped me tremendously—David's ruthless honesty with God. He had a heart that loved God, worshipped God, adored God, pursued God, but was also ruthlessly honest with God.

Only a heart that is in intimate relationship with God can be both a worshipping heart and an honest heart. It does not deny pain and evil. It does not overlook sin and shame. David loved God with reckless abandon, but he was also ruthlessly honest with God in those moments of life when sorrow and pain came flooding into his heart.

The challenge is we have grown up and live in a society that prizes itself in fixing anything, which is not a bad thing, except when you try to fix the unfixable. Life rarely follows the plotline we had so carefully constructed.

> We experience soaring success in one scene.
> And we experience stunning setback in another.
> Our hearts swell with hope and enthusiasm when the
>      giant lays slain.
> But what happens when a crisis strikes?
> When there is a loss you cannot recover from?
> When there is a pain that refuses to go away?
> When the tomorrow you imagined has vanished and is
>      not coming back?
> When your lost lines start to fade and disappear?

David faced many such situations. Before he became a king, he spent quite a bit of time in the wilderness. After he became a king, because of his son's rebellion, he ends up in the wilderness again.

And sometimes God does His best work in us in the wilderness, when the trappings of denial and earthly security and the neatly constructed plotlines of our stories are gone.

In these moments, David turned his heart's deepest anguish and pain toward God. He didn't minimize it, but he spoke it, named it, and then decided to still trust His God with it.

Let's walk you through some scenes from David's story.

> How long, LORD? Will you forget me
> forever? How long will you hide your face from
> me? . . . But I trust in your unfailing love.
>                                        —Psalm 13:1, 5

You have rejected us, God, and burst
upon us; you have been angry—now restore us!

*—Psalm 60:1*
*(he wrote this in the middle of a fierce battle)*


I have come into the deep waters; the
floods engulf me. I am worn out calling for help;
my throat is parched. My eyes fail, looking for
my God.

*—Psalm 69:2–3*
*(written in the middle of deep affliction)*


My flesh and my heart may fail, but God
is the strength of my heart and my portion forever.

*—Psalm 73:26*


Even in the midst of his darkest moments and most stunning failures, David lays it all out in front of God.

Loss, pain, anguish, and sorrow makes us question the very essence of God and the meaning, value, implication, and the very existence of our lost lines. And yet, when I ask people the periods of time when they grew the most in their walk with Jesus, without fail, people say it was in this pain, in this dark night, in the wilderness. That's when the roots grow deep and strong, faith is tested and forged, and the noise and chatter subsides and disappears long enough for us to ponder what we are building our lives on.

We gain a deeper sense of empathy with others and a depth of maturity in our faith. James says as much:

> Consider it a great joy, my brothers, whenever you experience various trials, knowing that the testing of your faith produces endurance. But endurance must do its complete work, so that you may be mature and complete, lacking nothing.
>
> —*James 1:2–4 HCSB*

Peter goes on to say in 1 Peter 1:6–7 that trials come so that our faith can be purified like gold is purified through fire. There is a payoff coming on the other side if we hang on. Our faith, our character, our relationship with brothers and sisters in Christ are things we will be carrying all the way into eternity.

Job was a man who lost everything—his family, his home, and his business. He went through the worst wilderness anyone can imagine. The Book of Job is basically Job trying to come to grips with his reality. He couldn't imagine why his fortunes had turned against him. He thought he was living his lost lines. And now this? After voicing his deep distress he said, "Isn't it clear that . . . God is sovereign, that He holds all things in His hand—every living soul, yes, every breathing creature?" (Job 12:9–10 *The Message*).

In my eight days of silence, I felt God speaking to me through David and Job. Even in this trial, even with my voice completely gone, isn't it clear that God is sovereign? And that He holds me, little insignificant me, a vapor of a life, a blade of grass, in His hands?

He is still here and He is still at work. Throughout Scripture, God says again and again, do not be afraid, I am with you. Even in those moments when the Line-Giver feels distant, disengaged, and disinterested, He is sovereign.

Job knew this, and in the next few verses he enumerated all the ways God works and is active and is intimately connected and involved and working in our world and in our lives. He used words like God is *leading* and *making* and *taking* and *overthrowing* and *silencing* and *pouring* and *disarming* and *revealing* and *bringing* and *destroying*.

We don't always see God's hand because our Line-Giver has the big picture in mind. He is at work even in those moments when He seems to hide from us and make us wait. And so in the next chapter, Job goes on to utter one of the greatest statements of faith ever made.

> Though he slay me, yet will I hope in him.
> —*Job 13:15*

So I read Job's words and decided I would likewise put my trust in God. I want to especially invite you into that place of trust if you are going through a deep struggle today, this very moment. Will you decide right now?

> **God is sovereign.**
> **He is my Line-Giver.**
> **There are things happening in my life right now that**
> **don't make sense.**
> **But I choose to still trust, still obey, still hope.**
> **I will throw myself at God's mercy—even if You slay me,**
> **yet will I hope in You.**

I remember praying in that week. *Even if I am never able to talk again, You will still be my Lord; You will still be my God.* I felt a deep sense of peace. That doesn't mean things got easy or were perfect. Doubts and questions remained. It did for Job. It does for me. It will for you.

In the very next chapter, right after putting his full trust in God, Job lays out his doubts, his questions, and his frustrations. He, like David, was ruthlessly honest with God. Job's friends tried to tell Job why he was experiencing hardship. And like Job's friends, sometimes we can be so glib with pat answers. Job said he spoke of things he did not understand. We should memorize those words. The point is, the book never really provides an answer. What it does say is that in those moments when our days don't make sense, the Line-Giver invites us to trust His wisdom and His sovereignty and His ultimate plan.

After eight days of not being able to speak, I went back to the hospital. There was zero improvement. There were three possibilities. Two would mean I would never be able to speak again. The third would mean a gradual recovery. Lots of people were praying. I went through another procedure (which, quite literally, was a real pain in the neck). But it sort of jump-started my vocal cords. I was able to utter my first words in eight days.

The weird thing is that the procedure restored all my high tones but not my normal voice at first. So the doctor said, "You know, you can talk and preach in high tones!" And I answered, "I am not preaching in falsetto!"

Slowly, my voice returned. But my vocal strength was only at about 60 percent. If through speech therapy it didn't get better, I would have to go back for the same procedure to jump-start my vocal cords once every three months for years. I was *not* looking forward to that.

Again, there was a lot of praying and fasting. I had to go through months of speech therapy, and now I am at 95 percent. I didn't have to go back for any further procedures.

Trusting God fully doesn't mean we silence our cries of anguish, our outbursts of fear, our doubts and our questions and our frustrations with God. It means we know who the Author of our lost lines is, and we unabashedly put our trust in Him. It means we know He is here and with us even when we cannot see Him.

Paul puts it this way:

We pray that you'll have the strength
to stick it out over the long haul—not the grim
strength of gritting your teeth but the glory-
strength God gives. It is strength that endures the
unendurable and spills over into joy, thanking the
Father who makes us strong enough to take part in
everything bright and beautiful that he has for us.
—*Colossians 1:11–12 The Message*

The wilderness changes us.
Our perspective changes,
our faith deepens,
our heart transforms as we are reminded that we are not
     sovereign, God is.
We pray,
we cry,
we plead,
we beg,
we get disoriented,
we get angry,
but when we let God, we are able to endure,
and somehow the next scene emerges from the ruins.
And we rise from the ashes,
stronger and bolder,
having had the trivial and the superficial washed off
    our souls.

*Chapter 18*

# STEP FORWARD

Be on your guard; stand firm in the faith;
be courageous; be strong. Do everything in love.
—*1 Corinthians 16:13–14*

Sometimes I wonder about my life. I lead
a small life . . . and sometimes I wonder, do I do it
because I like it or because I haven't been brave?
—*Kathleen Kelly, as portrayed by Meg Ryan,*
*You've Got Mail, written by*
*Nora Ephron and Miklós László*

Some time back, I was driving home from church, and
it was after a particularly hard week. It was evening,
and I was mulling over a speech I was thinking of making
to my two older girls, both in their teens. They are amazing girls,
exceptionally gifted, unpretentious, and respectful. Having grown
up in the church, they have participated in various ministries both in
and outside the church, especially in the arts and music.

A man who only occasionally attended our church made
a comment to me about my girls. I was preaching a series and
had asked them to sing a closing song. They had nailed it. It was

powerful and anointed. After the service, the man said something like this, "It must be wonderful for your daughters to have their dad be a pastor so they can have all these opportunities to be in front." Then he went on to say how my girls were in the Christmas play and the children's ministries play and so on.

So I fumbled a reply and said how they serve in multiple capacities behind the scenes. They have made sacrifices and gone on mission trips. I pointed out that this was a special song they sang once in the last nine months! We have so many gifted volunteers in our church that serve in multiple capacities. The man quickly backtracked.

So as I sat in my driveway, I started thinking maybe the man was right. Maybe I should tell my girls to dial it down a bit. That they should be less engaged in the church. That there are people who may not be as secure in who they are and their giftings and their abilities, and it is important to be mindful of them.

And it hit me—the speech I had been formulating in my mind was the worst speech I could ever give as a father. I, who talk about living our lost lines, was about to tell my girls that they needed to live their lost lines *giving it a lot less than their very best!* And how the cynical speech of one occasional visitor drowned out the voices of a hundred others who felt differently.

So I walked in, and in that instant, I flipped the script. Instead, I told my girls:

> As long as you stay rooted and grounded in Jesus,
> as long as you know where your gifts come from,
> as long as you know your light is a reflection of a far
> greater light,
> shine with full wattage. And never, ever apologize for it.

You should, of course, pay attention to others and their feedback, especially those who love you and have made deposits in your life, but don't allow anyone to convince you that you need to back down on being the person God created you to be.

> And as you walk this life there will be people who will
>         whisper doubts in your ears,
> there will be people who will try and put a cloud of
>         discouragement on your gifts,
> there will be people who will try to throw a towel or a
>         bucket of cynicism over your light,
> this world will try to beat you down.
> If you are going to live your lost lines, there will be
>         people who will say silly, crazy, stupid things to
>         make you back down, to make you shine less, to
>         make you be less than who you were meant to be.
> Don't listen to them.
> Don't allow their words to travel past your outer ears.
> Don't give them a neuron worth of thought.
> Don't back down.
> Don't give an inch.
> Don't shine any less.
> Don't turn the dimmer switch to the left on your light.
>         That's no good.
> The middle is no good either. Turn it fully to the right.
> *Shine as fiercely bright for Jesus as you can.*

It is easy to shrink back, to pull the covers over the life you were meant to live, to not offend anyone, to never seek or live out your lost lines, and when you do that, you make a decision to live some other lines— lukewarm, boring lines that are not offensive to the critics and the cynics. If you decide to find and live your lost lines, if you decide to craft a life after the calling of the Line-Giver, don't expect everyone to get in on it. Some will misinterpret what you are doing, some will ascribe made-up motives to you, and others will try to dissuade you, discourage you, and derail you. So it's easy to stay apathetic. *Apathy* is another word for the living dead.

The point is, you have to be comfortable with criticism, with being misunderstood, with being teased. But if you get all in and truly embark on a journey with the Line-Giver with full devotion, you will have so much love and joy and peace and, dare I say, fun, you will not have much time for the people who want to pull you down.

Don't live your lost lines with a lukewarm heart. Let it burn bright and white hot with passion. Let your soul pulsate with the realization that you are inhabiting the story that was written for you. Let your mind be renewed and captivated by the beauty and the majesty and the glory and the call of the Line-Giver.

Stay in the groove with the One who wants to breathe fresh life in you. God knows we need the light to glow intensely in a world so full of darkness. Which is why Jesus told us to shine brightly before people so they may see God's work in and through us and glorify Him (Matthew 5:16).

Yes, pride is a problem, but in more than two decades of my ministry, the far bigger problem I see in the church of Jesus Christ is God's people tepidly shining their light, apologetically using their gifts, and trying to practice a mutilated form of humility that doesn't advance the cause of Christ.

A whole lot of people often underuse or never use their God-given talents to their full potential out of fear. But the Master of the Talents is coming back, and He will want an accounting of what you did with the gifts you were given.

Whatever your lost lines are, you have been blessed with the right personality, talents, and ability to live it in all its fullness.

Living our lost lines is a decision between connecting or
    averting,
between being engaged or being consumed,
between charting the course with your Line-Giver or
    drifting along.
It will not always be easy.
It will take time.
It will take deliberate practice.
It will take attention and skill and effort.

So,
*What are you going to do with this precious gift of your
    one and only amazing life?*
You can allow the pettiness of some to shrink your vision
    and drain your passion.
You can ignore the low frequency signal of your soul.
You can sail along on low wattage.
You can keep close to the shore.
You can seek out a life of pleasure and comfort.

Or,
You can immerse yourself in the narrative of the Line-
    Giver.
Daily denying yourself from the lure of the script of this
    world.
Taking on the yoke of Christ.
Living as part of His community.
Asking deep questions and learning and discovering and
    growing.

It will change everything:

The way you live and work, the things you buy, the
decisions you make, the relationships you cultivate,
how you use your time and resources.

All the little decisions will impact the whole.

And a new life will emerge.

It's a decision.

You stand at the doorway to a whole new way of living.

Each day, *this day*, is a gift to join in the grand adventure
of living your lost lines.

Take a deep breath.

And step forward.

Be strong and courageous. Do not be afraid; do not be discouraged, for the LORD your God will be with you wherever you go.

—*Joshua 1:9*

I pray that the eyes of your heart may be enlightened in order that you may know the hope to which he has called you, the riches of his glorious inheritance in his holy people, and his incomparably great power for us who believe. That power is the same as the mighty strength he exerted when he raised Christ from the dead and seated him at his right hand in the heavenly realms, far above all rule and authority, power and dominion, and every name that is invoked, not only in the present age but also in the one to come. And God placed all things under his feet and appointed him to be head over everything for the church, which is his body, the fullness of him who fills everything in every way.

—*Ephesians 1:18–23*

There is no passion to be found playing small—in settling for a life that's less than the one you are capable of living.

—*Nelson Mandela*

# STUDY GUIDE

In the following pages you'll find questions to help you go deeper as a small group, reading group, or in your personal study. The goal here is not that you come up with a right answer but to create a space where you allow some time for introspection and reflection and be open to the nudging and whispers of the Holy Spirit. Listen closely—your lost lines are waiting to be found.

# CHAPTER 1
# GIVEN

Have you ever browsed the covers of men's and women's magazines? What overarching message do they transmit?

Raj covers several demographics—children, teens, men, and women—in his argument about how media shapes our story. Which one surprised you? Which didn't?

What messages shaped your story?

## CHAPTER 2
## ACHE

Raj argues that each of our souls emits a low-frequency signal calling us to live our lost lines. Do you agree? Why or why not?

Think back to some of the most soul-fulfilling things you've ever done in your life. What were these things? Can you decode any common thread running through them?

What makes you happiest?

# CHAPTER 3
# DISCONNECT

Do you experience a gap between your Sundays and your weekdays? Why does his happen to so many of us?

Read Romans 12. Which of Paul's instructions are easy for you? Which are hard?

What are some ways spiritual cognitive dissonance affects people? How do you think they resolve it? How do you resolve it?

## CHAPTER 4
## MASKS

In what ways do you think the idea of personal branding grows and/or hinders us from being who we were created to be?

Think back on person and persona and the story of Ananias and Sapphira. Why do we struggle so much with matching our person and persona?

Read Luke 12:1–12 and 2 Corinthians 4 in multiple versions. How can we avoid the lure and trap of putting on a false persona?

# CHAPTER 5
## TUNING IN

What part of your week or daily routine is most frustrating or hard for you?

How can you tune in to the channel of God's life-giving presence in those moments?

Read the following parts of the Christmas narrative: Luke 1:26–38; Luke 2:1–7; Matthew 2:13–16; and Matthew 2:19–21. What do you think helped Joseph and Mary stay centered and obedient and faithful through it all?

## CHAPTER 6
## THE LINE-GIVER

Raj traced the history of how we got and lost our lines and how we can find them again. Which part of this biblical narrative arc stood out to you?

Do you know people who found Christ and then their stories were completely transformed? What about your story? How was your story transformed by the Line-Giver?

Raj says joining our Line-Giver in His mission to transform our lives, our homes, our families, our communities, our nation, and our world is the greatest mission ever given to humans. Do you agree? Why or why not?

# CHAPTER 7
# DIVIDED

Read the story of Amaziah in 2 Kings 14 and 2 Chronicles 25. Why did Amaziah not follow God wholeheartedly? Do people still do this? What is the danger of a divided heart?

Raj says whenever we are in drift mode, we are usually not drifting in the right direction. Do you agree? Have you ever drifted? What causes people to drift? How can we stay on course?

Go over the list of indications listed in chapter 7 that can predict whether a person is living their lost lines or not. Which ones do you struggle with the most?

# CHAPTER 8
# HEART

Why does the Bible tells us to guard our hearts above all else? How do you consciously guard your heart?

How can we have a heart like David's?

What does having a heart that is wide-open to God mean? Why is that so essential in us finding our lost lines?

# CHAPTER 9
## SIMULCAST

Why does the Bible intricately lock in the themes of hearing and obeying? How can we avoid being hearers who aren't doers?

Read the parable of the sower in Matthew 13:3–9. How can we learn to be the fertile soil?

What are some ways the Sower "broadcasts" our lost lines?

# CHAPTER 10
## AMAZED

How is it possible to live in our world today without amazement? What would living in amazement look like for you?

What causes boredom? Have you ever gone through long seasons of boredom? How did you overcome it?

People encountering Jesus were left amazed. How can we gain that sense of amazement?

# CHAPTER 11
# DISCOVERY

Read all the verses discussed in this chapter that talk about calling to God. What do they say about our Line-Giver? What do they say about what kind of posture we are to adopt toward Him?

Raj outlines three ways to live that helps us discover our lost lines—calling to God, recognizing Jesus as the Author of our lost lines and staying close to Him, and expanding our awareness of God's current activity in and around us. Which one is easiest for you? Which one is hardest?

In the last page of this chapter, there is a list of things we all do on a regular basis. What would doing those things *with Jesus* look like?

# CHAPTER 12
# ZONES

Do you agree that there is a massive relentless human tendency to flatten individuals into neat little categories? How does this play out in your circles of influence?

What was Jesus' attitude toward zoning people? How can we adopt His mindset and attitude?

Have you ever been zoned? How did that make you feel? What can you do to dismantle the barriers of zoning between people?

# CHAPTER 13
# RENEWING

Paul says there is a war raging against our minds (Romans 7:23). What does this mean? What does this mean for you?

What kind of intentional holy habits can help us create the space and time needed for the Holy Spirit to renew our minds?

What does it mean to have the mind of Christ? Why is that important to us finding our lost lines?

# CHAPTER 14
## CONNECT

Raj argues that prayer is living in ambient awareness of our Line-Giver. Do you agree?

Why is prayer so crucial to discovering and living our lost lines?

How can you adopt the posture of prayer and the outline of the Lord's Prayer into your life?

# CHAPTER 15
# ENSEMBLE

What did you think about the Japanese CEO's comment, "our hearts aren't touching"? Is this a problem in America? How so?

Why is the community of Christ so crucial to us discovering and living our lost lines?

How can you deepen relational connects? How will this help you and others live out our lost lines?

## CHAPTER 16
## RETAKES

How does Jonah's story help us understand our Line-Giver's response to when we fail to live out our lines?

What can we learn from our retakes?

Why is the "chapter 2" of confession and repentance necessary for the "chapter 3" of retakes?

## CHAPTER 17
## ENDURING

Raj writes that God often does not reveal the next scene until we have lived the current one well. Do you agree? Have you ever personally experienced this?

Have you ever gone through (or are currently going through) a tough situation where everything seemed lost? How would the prayer of Job help?

Raj says the wilderness changes us. What are some ways it can change us for the better? For worse? What are some wilderness moments you have experienced?

# CHAPTER 18
## STEP FORWARD

Have thoughtless or petty remarks ever stopped you from doing something bold and brave?

Share about a situation where the uplifting words of someone gave you much-needed wind in your sails.

Raj argues that pride can be a problem but that the greater problem in the church is God's people tepidly shining their light, being apologetic about using their gifts, trying to practice a mutilated form of humility that doesn't advance the cause of Christ. How do you see this belief unfolding in your church?

# BIBLIOGRAPHY

Barclay, William. *The New Daily Study Bible: The Gospel of Luke.* Kentucky: Westminster John Knox Press, 2001.

Barth, Karl, quoted in Mark Galli, "Non-Orthodoxy: Karl Barth," *Christianity Today*, accessed March 8, 2018, http://www.christianity today.com/history/issues/issue-65/neo-orthodoxy-karl-barth .html.

"Beauty at Any Cost," YWCA, accessed March 7, 2018, http://www.ywca .org/atf/cf/%7B711d5519-9e3c-4362-b753-ad138b5d352c%7D /BEAUTY-AT-ANY-COST.PDF.

Bonhoeffer, Dietrich. *Life Together: The Classic Exploration of Christian in Community.* California: HarperOne, 2009.

Boorstin, Daniel J. *The Image: Or, What Happened to the American Dream.* New York: Antheneum Books, 1962.

Carpenter, Francis Bicknell. *Six Months at the White House with Abraham Lincoln.* Massachusetts: Applewood Books, 1866.

Chesterton, G. K., *Heretics*, quoted in John Hambrick, *Move Toward the Mess: The Ultimate Fix for a Boring Christian Life* (Colorado Springs, CO: David C Cook, 2016).

Colin, Chris, "The Incredibly True Story of Renting a Friend in Tokyo," *Afar*, February 19, 2016, https://www.afar.com/magazine /the-incredibly-true-story-of-renting-a-friend-in-tokyo.

"The Common Sense Census: Media Use By Tweens and Teens," Common Sense, accessed March 7, 2018, https://www .commonsensemedia.org/sites/default/files/uploads/research /census_executivesummary.pdf.

Cummings, E. E. *E. E. Cummings: A Miscellany Revised.* New York: October House, 1965.

da Vinci, Leonardo, quoted in Andy Zubko, *Treasury of Spiritual Wisdom: A Collection of 10,000 Inspirational Quotations* (Delhi, India: Motilal Banarsidass Publishers, 2004), 317.

Doctorow, E. L., quoted in Robert Andrews, *The New Penguin Dictionary of Modern Quotations* (London, England: Penguin Group, 2003).

Du Bos, Charles, quoted in Rod Stryker, *The Four Desires: Creating a Life of Purpose, Happiness, Prosperity, and Freedom* (New York, NY: Random House, 2011), 5.

Duhigg, Charles. *The Power of Habit: Why We Do What We Do in Life and Business*. Canada: Doubleday Canada, 2012

Eldredge, John. *Wild at Heart*. Tennessee: Thomas Nelson, 2001.

Entis, Laura, "Chronic Loneliness Is a Modern-Day Epidemic," Fortune, June 22, 2016, http://fortune.com/2016/06/22 /loneliness-is-a-modern-day-epidemic/.

Fabio, Santa, "Generation Y's goals? Wealth and fame," *USA Today*, January 10, 2007, http://usatoday30.usatoday.com/news /nation/2007-01-09-gen-y-cover_x.htm.

"Gates Foundation: Giving a Fortune Away," YouTube video, 13:32, from an episode of *60 Minutes*, televised by CBS on October 3, 2010, posted by CBS, October 3, 2010, https://www.youtube .com/watch?v=2VdMqmVtnOM.

Gates, Melinda, "What nonprofits can learn from Coca-Cola," filmed September 2010 at TEDxChange, New York, NY, video, 16:22, https://www.ted.com/talks/melinda_french_gates_what _nonprofits_can_learn_from_coca_cola#t-926803.

Graslie, Serrie, "The Modern American Man, Charted," National Public Radio, July 17, 2014, https://www.npr.org/2014/07/17/326175817 /the-modern-american-man-charted.

Hammarskjöld, Dag, quoted in Michiko Kakutani, "Books of the Times: A Test of Faith for a Father Who Longs for Grace" (*The*

*New York Times*, November 28, 1995, http://www.nytimes
.com/1995/11/28/books/books-of-the-times-a-test-of-faith-for
-a-father-who-longs-for-grace.html).

Hawthorne, Nathaniel. *The Scarlet Letter*. New York: Bantam Classics,
1981.

Heschel, Abraham Joshua. *God in Search of Man: A Philosophy of
Judaism*. New York: Farrar, Straus and Giroux, 1976.

Hurston, Zora Neale. *Dust Tracks on a Road*. Kansas: Tandem Library,
1996.

Ingraham, Christopher, "The American commute is worse today
than it's ever been," *The Washington Post*, February 22, 2017,
https://www.washingtonpost.com/news/wonk/wp/2017/02/22
/the-american-commute-is-worse-today-than-its-ever-been
/?utm_term=.038cde338027.

Keller, Hellen, "Three Days to See," *The Atlantic*, January 1933,
https://www.theatlantic.com/past/docs/issues/33jan/keller.htm.

Kierkegaard, Søren, *Parables of Kierkegaard*, ed. Thomas C. Oden
(New Jersey: Princeton University Press, 1978).

Kierkegaard, Søren, *Two Ages: The Age of Revolution and the Present
Age*, trans. and ed. Howard V. Hong and Edna H. Hong (New
Jersey: Princeton University Press, 1978).

King, Martin Luther, Jr. *The Measure of a Man*. Connecticut: Martino
Fine Books, 2013.

Kuyper, Abraham, quoted in Doug Gay, *Honey from the Lion: Christian
Theology and the Ethics of Nationalism* (London, England: SCM
Press, 2013), 132.

Lewis, C. S. *Mere Christianity*. California: HarperOne, 2015.

Linn, Susan. *Consuming Kids: Protecting Our Children from the
Onslaught of Marketing and Advertising*. New York: Anchor
Books, 2004.

Mandela, Nelson, quoted in John C. Maxwell, *No Limits: Blow the CAP off Your Capacity* (Nashville, TN: Center Street Publishing, 2017).

May, Rollo. *The Cry for Myth*. New York: W. W. Norton and Company, 1991.

Nouwen, Henri. *Life of the Beloved: Spiritual Living in a Secular World.* New York: The Crossroad Publishing Company, 1992.

Nouwen, Henri. *The Road to Daybreak: A Spiritual Journey.* New York: Doubleday, 1990.

Postman, Neil. *Amusing Ourselves to Death: Public Discourse in the Age of Show Business*. London, England: Penguin Books, 2005.

Ravenhill, Leonard. *Why Revival Tarries*. Minnesota: Bethany House, 1987.

Roller, Emma, "Your Facts or Mine?," *The New York Times*, October 25, 2016, https://www.nytimes.com/2016/10/25/opinion/campaign -stops/your-facts-or-mine.html?mcubz=3.

Saint Anthony, quoted in Brian Zahnd, *Sinners in the Hands of a Loving God: The Scandalous Truth of the Very Good News* (New York, NY: WaterBrook, 2017), 138.

Sayers, Dorothy L. *Letters to a Diminished Church: Passionate Arguments for the Relevance of Christian Doctrine*. Tennessee: Thomas Nelson, 2004.

Schor, Juliet. *Born to Buy: The Commercialized Child and the New Consumer Culture*. New York: Simon and Schuster, 2014.

Seneca. *On the Shortness of Life*, trans. C. D. N. Costa (New York: Penguin Group, 2004).

Sheehy, Gail. *New Passages: Mapping Your Life Across Time*. New York: Random House, 1996.

"Small Life," *You've Got Mail*, directed by Nora Ephron (1998; Warner Bros.).

Smedes, Lewis. *Forgive and Forget: Healing the Hurts We Don't Deserve*. New York: HarperCollins, 1984.

Story, Louise, "Anywhere the Eye Can See, It's Likely to See an Ad," *The New York Times*, January 15, 2007, http://www.nytimes.com /2007/01/15/business/media/15everywhere.html ?pagewanted=all&_r=0.

Tefilah, Mishkan, *Jewish Sabbath Prayer Book*, quoted in Terry Hershey, *The Power of Pause: Becoming More by Doing Less* (Chicago, IL: Loyola Press, 2009).

Thompson, Clive, "Brave New World of Digital Intimacy," *The New York Times*, September 5, 2008, http://www.nytimes.com/2008/09/07 /magazine/07awareness-t.html.

Thompson, Derek, "Lotteries: America's $70 Billion Shame," *The Atlantic*, May 11, 2015, https://www.theatlantic.com/business /archive/2015/05/lotteries-americas-70-billion-shame/392870/.

Tolkien, J. R. R. *The Fellowship of the Ring*. Massachusetts: Mariner Books, 2012.

Tolstoy, Leo. *Anna Karenina*. London, England: Penguin Books, 2002.

Twain, Mark. *Adventures of Huckleberry Finn*. Delaware: Prestwick House, 2005.

Voskamp, Ann. *One Thousand Gifts: A Dare to Live Fully Right Where You Are*. Michigan: Zondervan, 2011.

Willard, Dallas. *Hearing God Through the Year: A 365-Day Devotional*. Illinois: InterVarsity Press, 2004.

Willard, Dallas. *The Spirit of Disciplines: Understanding How God Changes Lives*. California: HarperOne, 1999.

"Women in the Labor Force in 2010," United States Department of Labor, accessed March 7, 2018, https://www.dol.gov/wb /factsheets/qf-laborforce-10.htm.

**If you enjoyed this book, will you consider sharing the message with others?**

Let us know your thoughts at info@newhopepublishers.com.
You can also let the author know by visiting or sharing a photo of the cover on our social media pages or leaving a review at a retailer's site. All of it helps us get the message out!
Twitter.com/NewHopeBooks
Facebook.com/NewHopePublishers
Instagram.com/NewHopePublishers

---

New Hope® Publishers is an imprint of Iron Stream Media, which derives its name from Proverbs 27:17, "As iron sharpens iron, so one person sharpens another."

---

For more information on ISM and New Hope Publishers, please visit
IronStreamMedia.com
NewHopePublishers.com

This sharpening describes the process of discipleship, one to another. With this in mind, Iron Stream Media provides a variety of solutions for churches, missionaries, and nonprofits ranging from in-depth Bible study curriculum and Christian book publishing to custom publishing and consultative services. Through the popular Life Bible Study and Student Life Bible Study brands, ISM provides web-based full-year and short-term Bible study teaching plans as well as printed devotionals, Bibles, and discipleship curriculum.

# Also by
# RAJ PILLAI...

## UNEARTHED

DISCOVER LIFE AS GOD'S
*Masterpiece*

RAJ PILLAI

# GIFTS OF HOPE SERIES

THE GIFTS OF HOPE SERIES offers hope to those walking through some of life's most challenging circumstances. Each book offers thirty devotionals, Scripture, and prayers that provide readers inspiration and encouragement.

## Each only $9.99

# OTHER NEW RELEASES FROM
# NEW HOPE

Unshakable
PURSUIT
Chasing the God Who Chases Us

GRACE THORNTON

$9.99

Leading Through the Storms

Anchored

Cynthia
Cavanaugh

$14.99

The Power in Wilderness Journeys

THE
WAYWARD
WAY

TAYLOR FIELD
AUTHOR OF THE UPSIDE-DOWN SERIES

$14.99

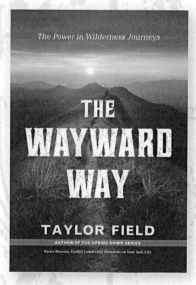

UNHITCHING
from the CRAZY
TRAIN

Finding Rest in a World
You Can't Control

JULIE SPARKMAN
WITH JENNIFER PHILLIPS

$14.99

VISIT **NEWHOPEPUBLISHERS.COM**
FOR MORE INFORMATION.